COUNSELS
on Agriculture

From the writings of Ellen G. White

Compiled by John Dysinger

TEACH Services, Inc.
PUBLISHING
www.TEACHServices.com • (800) 367-1844

All scripture quotations are from the King James Version.

World rights reserved. This book or any portion thereof may not be copied or reproduced in any form or manner whatever, except as provided by law, without the written permission of the publisher, except by a reviewer who may quote brief passages in a review.

The author assumes full responsibility for the accuracy of all facts and quotations as cited in this book. The opinions expressed in this book are the author's personal views and interpretations, and do not necessarily reflect those of the publisher.

This book is provided with the understanding that the publisher is not engaged in giving spiritual, legal, medical, or other professional advice. If authoritative advice is needed, the reader should seek the counsel of a competent professional.

Copyright © 2016 TEACH Services, Inc.

ISBN-13: 978-1-4796-0638-2 (Paperback)

ISBN-13: 978-1-4796-0639-9 (ePub)

ISBN-13: 978-1-4796-0640-5 (Mobi)

Library of Congress Control Number: 2016903510

Published by

TEACH Services, Inc.
PUBLISHING
www.TEACHServices.com • (800) 367-1844

To the Reader

"In God's plan for Israel every family had a home on the land, with sufficient ground for tilling. Thus were provided both the means and the incentive for a useful, industrious, and self-supporting life. And *no devising of men has ever improved upon that plan*. To the world's departure from it is owing, to a large degree, the poverty and wretchedness that exist today" (MH 183, emphasis added).[1]

This is *the* quote that compelled my family and me to leave the "standard American life" and embark on the adventure of agriculture. If an agrarian life was God's ideal plan, then that's what we wanted! There have been lots of bumps, falls, twists and turns in the intervening 17 years, but we can honestly say we have no regrets about that choice.

When we started, our oldest child was not even 7; now she is 23 and married! Our four sons are now young men. I can't imagine a better place to raise children than on a farm. Although we had no idea what we were getting into when we started, and although we have made plenty of mistakes along the way, God has blessed us amazingly!

It has taken years for us to even begin to comprehend how all-encompassing the blessings of agriculture are. As I often remind my family, "It's not just about growing good food." It's about health: spiritual, mental, physical, emotional, social, moral.... There are very good reasons why God put man in a garden!

As we began experiencing the benefits of agriculture, we had a growing desire to share these blessings with others. One way I wanted to share was to put together a compilation of Ellen G. White's quotes on the subject. I felt if people saw all that this inspired writer had to say on agriculture, they would have to acknowledge its importance and take appropriate actions. That was many years ago.... But, well, let's just say that farm life is busy.

In the fall of 2011, my brother (and farm partner) and his family generously offered to cover the farm while our family took some time off. This was the opportunity I needed! After spending a week at Andrews University (Berrien Springs, MI) looking for unpublished Ellen White quotes on agriculture, we headed to Honduras for an amazing, God-directed, three-month sabbatical. It was there that the bulk of this compilation was completed. But that was in 2011! Well—did I say that farm life is busy?

---

1. Please see the Bibliography on page 181 for a key to these reference abbreviations.

A couple years ago I returned to Andrews for another week of research—hoping to put the finishing touches on the project. But, I felt like I was trying to uncover an iceberg—there were always new quotes surfacing with no end in sight.

Then, just a few weeks ago, my dear wife told me she was sending me away to finish this project. I told her I didn't think I could do it—after all, we were in the middle of our farming season. But she is a very driven women and she, along with my wonderful family and some amazing apprentices, have managed the farm quite well without me.

As I have re-immersed myself in this project, I have been re-impressed with how important this topic is. This is not my project; this is God's project! This is His inspired counsel for the times we are living in. Everyone needs to read this! Agriculture is not just a hobby or an elective; it is an *essential* (her word, not mine). My prayer is that you will be convicted and compelled to action by what you read.

Just a few words of explanation about the construction of this compilation:

1. My original intent was for this to be an exhaustive compilation of everything Mrs. White had to say about agriculture. Well, that exhaustive quest turned into an exhausting one. Many keywords had multiple thousands of search hits—and then there were the many slightly different versions of the same quote. I now make no claims to have an exhaustive compilation, but I think it's pretty close. I am sure there are some hidden gems still waiting to be uncovered. If you find them, I'd love to hear from you!

2. It was my goal to get back to the original sources for all the quotes compiled—so readers could more easily research the context. I believe this has been largely accomplished—with a few exceptions where later variations seemed more appropriate.

3. Since this compilation is on agriculture, I chose to *only* use quotes that had agricultural terminology included. This left out *many* quotes dealing with manual labor, industry, outdoors, nature study, etc. where reference to agriculture was implied but not explicit. Again, there are a handful of exceptions.

4. The chapter divisions are arbitrary but seemed to logically emerge out of the quotes compiled. Although many of the quotations could have easily fit into more than one chapter, I chose the one I felt was most appropriate. *I have diligently sought to avoid duplications of the same quote.*

5. I endeavored to attach a date to every quote and have chosen to arrange them in chronological order within the subject area. Exceptions would be when Mrs. White reminisces about former days or where the subject matter fits better in a different order.

6. Every attempt has been made to include the reference just as it appears on the Ellen White online database—for easier further research.

7. This compilation is topical. I know of someone else who has been working on a chronological compilation of her writings on agriculture. I hope that will come to fruition because I think each has its place.

8. I have refrained from interjecting personal commentary into this compilation and have attempted to let the author speak for herself without my personal bias. The only exception would be that I have chosen some favorite "pull quotes" to emphasize throughout the book.

9. An inherent weakness of compilations is that they can take things out of their original context and often give an unbalanced view of the subject matter. I have endeavored to avoid these shortcomings. But, in this case, because the subject of agriculture has been so neglected, I make no apologies in overemphasizing it—with the hope of bringing it back into its proper balance.

It feels like this project, although only four years in the making, has spanned a whole technological revolution. My original research at Andrews was done using a typewritten card catalog and photocopied manuscripts. Then, in Honduras I used the Ellen White CD-ROM. Now I am finishing the project using the online research tool, www.egwwritings.org—which now (as of July 2015) has all her previously unpublished letters and manuscripts available at the click of a button! There's never been an easier time to study what this inspired writer had to say!

Although some may question the relevance of this volume in the 21st century, I believe it is present truth for this generation—and possibly more relevant than ever before! May it be the springboard for deeper and more thorough research into the topics presented. More importantly, may it inspire a new generation of farmers and gardeners!

John Dysinger
September 2015
Williamsport, TN

P.S. After spending considerable time recently searching the previously unpublished writings on the online database, I realize there may be more undiscovered jewels than I first imagined. I have added those I found, but now feel it is more urgent to get this out to the people than to have it more exhaustive.

Contents

God's Plan for Man 9

Promises for the Agriculturalist 19

A Call for Christian Farmers 22

Agriculture at Home. 36

Agriculture and Our Schools 47

Agriculture and Our Health Care Institutions 87

Agriculture for Ministers and Other Gospel Workers 98

Physical Benefits of Agriculture 102

Spiritual Lessons From Agriculture 107

Agriculture in the Last Days 157

Ellen White Led by Example 161

Bibliography 181

God's Plan for Man

The Original Garden
"I saw that the holy angels often visited the garden, and gave instruction to Adam and Eve concerning their employment" (1SG 20, 1858).

"God gave our first parents the food he designed that the race should eat. It was contrary to his plan to have the life of any creature taken. There was to be no death in Eden. The fruit of the trees in the garden, was the food man's wants required. God gave man no permission to eat animal food until after the flood" (4aSG 120, 1864).

"Although everything God had made was in the perfection of beauty, and there seemed nothing wanting upon the earth which God had created to make Adam and Eve happy, yet he manifested his great love to them by planting a garden especially for them. A portion of their time was to be occupied in the happy employment of dressing the garden, and a portion in receiving the visits of angels, listening to their instruction, and in happy meditation. Their labor was not wearisome, but pleasant and invigorating. This beautiful garden was to be their home, their special residence.

"In this garden the Lord placed trees of every variety for usefulness and beauty. There were trees laden with luxuriant fruit, of rich fragrance, beautiful to the eye, and pleasant to the taste, designed of God to be food for the holy pair. There were the lovely vines which grew upright, laden with their burden of fruit, unlike anything man had seen since the fall. The fruit was very large, and of different colors; some nearly black, some purple, red, pink and light green. This beautiful and luxuriant growth of fruit upon the branches of the vine was called grapes. They did not trail upon the ground, although not supported by trellises, but the weight of the fruit bowed them down. It was the happy labor of Adam and Eve to form beautiful bowers from the branches of the vine, and train them, forming dwellings of nature's beautiful, living trees and foliage, laden with fragrant fruit" (1SP 25, 1870).

"Even the great God is a lover of the beautiful. He has given us unmistakable evidence of this in the work of his hands. He planted for our first parents a beautiful garden in Eden. Stately trees were caused to grow out of the ground, of every description, for usefulness and ornament. The beautiful flowers were formed, of rare loveliness, of every tint and hue, perfuming the air. The merry songsters, of varied plumage, caroled forth their joyous songs to the praise of their Creator. It was the design of God that man should find happiness in the employment of tending the things he had created, and that his wants should be met with the fruits of the trees of the garden" (HR July 1, 1871).

"The Lord surrounded Adam and Eve in Paradise with everything that was useful and lovely. God planted for them a beautiful garden. No herb, nor flower, nor tree, was wanting, which might be for use and ornament. The Creator of man knew that this workmanship of his hands could not be happy without employment. Paradise delighted their souls, but this was not enough; they must have labor to call into exercise the organs of the body. The Lord had made them for use. If happiness consisted in doing nothing, man, in his state of holy innocence, would have been left unemployed. But He who formed man knew what would be for his best happiness, and he no sooner made him than he gave him his appointed work. In order to be happy, he must labor" (HR July 1, 1872).

"God prepared for Adam and Eve a beautiful garden. He provided for them everything their wants required. He planted for them trees of every variety, bearing fruit. With a liberal hand he surrounded them with his bounties—the trees, for usefulness and beauty, and the lovely flowers, which sprung up spontaneously, and flourished in rich profusion around them, were to know nothing of decay. Adam and Eve were rich indeed. They possessed beautiful Eden. Adam was monarch in this beautiful domain. None can question the fact that Adam was rich. But God knew that Adam could not be happy unless he had employment. Therefore he gave him something to do. He was to dress the garden.

"The Creator of man never designed that he should be idle. The Lord formed man out of the dust of the ground, and breathed into his nostrils the breath of life, and man became a living soul. It was the law of nature, therefore the law of God, that brain, nerve, and muscle, should be in active motion. Young gentlemen and ladies that refuse to labor because they are not compelled to, and because it is not fashionable, are not guided and controlled by enlightened reason. Those who shun manual labor, cannot have physical stamina. In order for the young to enjoy perfect health and perfect happiness, every organ and function must be in perfect operation as God designed they should be. If all the organs act their natural part, life, health, and happiness, will be the result. Too little exercise, and staying in-doors too much, will bring on feebleness and disease of some one or more of the organs. It is sinful to impair or weaken one of the powers God has given us. The great Creator designed that we should have perfect bodies, that we might preserve them in health, and render to him the offering of a living sacrifice, holy and acceptable to God.

"Exercise in useful labor will be carrying out the original plan of God, when he bade Adam and Eve to dress the garden. Life is precious, and should be preserved intelligently by regarding the laws of our being" (HR May 1, 1873).

"Many look upon work as a curse, originating with the enemy of souls. This is a mistaken idea. God gave labor to man as a blessing, to occupy his mind, to strengthen his body, and to develop his faculties. Adam toiled in the garden of Eden, and felt it to be one of the pleasures of his holy existence to do so. Later, when he was driven from his beautiful home, as the result of his disobedience, and was forced to struggle with a stubborn soil to gain his daily bread, that very labor, although far different from his pleasant occupation in the garden, was a relief to his sorrowing soul, a protection against temptation" (HR September 1, 1876).

> *"God gave labor to man as a blessing, to occupy his mind, to strengthen his body, and to develop his faculties."*

[Alternate version] "Many look upon useful labor as a curse originating with the enemy of souls; but this is a mistaken view. Judicious labor is indispensable to both the happiness and the prosperity of the race. God ordained it for man as a blessing, to occupy his mind, to strengthen his body, and to develop his faculties. Industry makes the feeble strong, the timid brave, the poor rich, and the wretched happy. Adam labored in the garden of Eden, and he found in mental and physical activity the highest pleasures of his holy existence. When, as the result of his disobedience, he was driven from that beautiful home, and was forced to struggle with a stubborn soil to gain his daily bread, that very labor was a relief to his sorrow and remorse, a safeguard against temptation" (ST November 12, 1885).

"Adam and Eve came forth from the hand of their Creator in the perfection of every physical, mental, and spiritual endowment. God planted for them a garden, and surrounded them with everything that was lovely and attractive to the eye, which their physical necessities required. This holy pair looked upon a world of unsurpassed loveliness and glory. A benevolent Creator had given them evidences of His goodness and love in providing them with fruits, vegetables, and grains, and in causing to grow out of the ground every variety of tree for usefulness and beauty.

"The holy pair looked upon nature as a picture of unsurpassed loveliness. The brown earth was clothed with a carpet of living green, diversified with an endless variety of self-perpetuating flowers. Shrubs, flowers, and trailing vines regaled the senses with their beauty and fragrance. The many varieties of lofty trees were laden with delicious fruit of every kind, adapted to please the taste and meet the wants of the happy Adam and Eve. This Eden home God provided for our first parents, giving them unmistakable evidences of His great love and care for them.

"Adam was crowned king in Eden. To him was given dominion over every living thing that God had created. The Lord blessed Adam and Eve with intelligence such as He had not given to any other creature. He made Adam the rightful sovereign over all the works of his hands. Man, made in the divine image, could contemplate and appreciate the glorious works of God in nature.

"Adam and Eve could trace the skill and glory of God in every spire of grass, and in every shrub and flower. The natural loveliness which surrounded them reflected like a mirror the wisdom, excellence, and love, of their Heavenly Father. And their songs of affection and praise rose sweetly and reverentially to heaven, harmonizing with the songs of the exalted angels, and with the happy birds who were caroling forth their music without a care. There was no disease, decay, nor death. Life was in everything the eye rested upon. The atmosphere was filled with life. Life was in every leaf, in every flower, and in every tree.

"The Lord knew that Adam could not be happy without labor; therefore, he gave him the pleasant employment of dressing the garden. And, as he tended the things of beauty and usefulness around him, he could behold the goodness and glory of God in his created works. Adam had themes for contemplation in the works of God in Eden, which was heaven in miniature. God did not form man merely to contemplate His glorious works; therefore, He gave him hands for labor, as well as a mind and heart for contemplation. If the happiness of man consisted in doing nothing, the Creator would not have given Adam his appointed work. Man was to find happiness in labor, as well as in meditation. Adam could take in the grand idea that he was created in the image of God, to be like him in righteousness and holiness. His mind was capable of continual cultivation, expansion, refinement, and noble elevation; for God was his teacher, and angels were his companions" (2Red 6, 7, 1877).

"The home of our first parents was to be a pattern for other homes as their children should go forth to occupy the earth. That home, beautified by the hand of God Himself, was not a gorgeous palace. Men, in their pride, delight in magnificent and costly edifices and glory in the works of their own hands; but God placed Adam in a garden. This was his dwelling. The blue heavens were its dome; the earth, with its delicate flowers and carpet of living green, was its floor; and the leafy branches of the goodly trees were its canopy. Its walls were hung with the most magnificent adornings—the handiwork of the great Master Artist. In the surroundings of the holy pair was a lesson for all time—that true happiness is found, not in the indulgence of pride and luxury, but in communion with God through His created works. If men would give less attention to the artificial, and would cultivate greater simplicity, they would come far nearer to answering the purpose of God in their creation. Pride and ambition are never satisfied, but those who are truly wise will find substantial and elevating pleasure in the sources of enjoyment that God has placed within the reach of all.

> *True happiness is found, not in the indulgence of pride and luxury, but in communion with God through His created works.*

"To the dwellers in Eden was committed the care of the garden, 'to dress it and to keep it.' Their occupation was not wearisome, but pleasant and invigorating. God appointed labor as a blessing to man, to occupy his mind, to strengthen his body, and to develop his faculties. In mental and physical activity Adam found one of the highest pleasures of his holy existence. And when, as a result of his disobedience, he was driven from his beautiful home, and forced to struggle with a stubborn soil to gain his daily bread, that very labor, although widely different from his pleasant occupation in the garden, was a safeguard against temptation and a source of happiness. Those who regard work as a curse, attended though it be with weariness and pain, are cherishing an error. The rich often look down with contempt upon the working classes, but this is wholly at variance with God's purpose in creating man. What are the possessions of even the most wealthy in comparison with the heritage given to the lordly Adam? Yet Adam was not to be idle. Our Creator, who understands what is for man's happiness, appointed Adam his work. The true joy of life is found only by the working men and women. The angels are diligent workers; they are the ministers of God to the children of men. The Creator has prepared no place for the stagnating practice of indolence" (PP 49, 50, 1890).

"God gave Adam and Eve employment. Eden was the school for our first parents, and God was their instructor. They learned how to till the soil and to care for the things which the Lord had planted. They did not regard labor as degrading, but as a great blessing. Industry was a pleasure to Adam and Eve. The fall of Adam changed the order of things; the earth was cursed; but the decree that man should earn his bread by the sweat of his brow was not given as a curse. Through faith and hope, labor was to be a blessing to the descendants of Adam and Eve" (Ms8a-1894).

"The Lord has given to every man his work. When the Lord created Adam and Eve it was not for their happiness to be idle. Activity is essential for happiness, and the Lord told Adam and Eve to till and dress the garden. In this work of agriculture our every faculty is brought into action" (Ms185-1898).

"God placed our first parents in Paradise, surrounding them with all that was useful and lovely. In their Eden home nothing was wanting that could minister to their comfort and happiness. And to Adam was given the work of caring for the garden. The Creator knew that Adam could not be happy without employment. The beauty of the garden delighted him, but this was not enough. He must have labor to call into exercise the wonderful organs of the body. Had happiness consisted in doing nothing, man, in his state of holy innocence, would have been left unemployed. But he who created man knew what would be for his happiness; and no sooner had he created him, than he gave him his appointed work. The promise of future glory, and the decree that man must toil for his daily bread, came from the same throne" (YI February 27, 1902).

"A life of useful labor is indispensable to the physical, mental, and moral well-being of man" (CTBH 96, 1890). (An alternate ending of the previous quote)

"It was not God's purpose that His people should be crowded into cities, huddled together in terraces and tenements. In the beginning He placed our first parents in a garden amidst the beautiful sights and attractive sounds of nature, and these sights and sounds He desires men to rejoice in today. The more nearly we come into harmony with God's original plan, the more favorable will be our position for the recovery and the preservation of health" (7T 87, 1902).

> *"The more nearly we come into harmony with God's original plan, the more favorable will be our position for the recovery and the preservation of health."*

"The system of education instituted at the beginning of the world was to be a model for man throughout all aftertime. As an illustration of its principles a model school was established in Eden, the home of our first parents. The Garden of Eden was the schoolroom, nature was the lesson book, the Creator Himself was the instructor, and the parents of the human family were the students....

"To Adam and Eve was committed the care of the garden, 'to dress it and to keep it.' Genesis 2:15. Though rich in all that the Owner of the universe could supply, they were not to be idle. Useful occupation was appointed them as a blessing, to strengthen the body, to expand the mind, and to develop the character.

"The book of nature, which spread its living lessons before them, afforded an exhaustless source of instruction and delight. On every leaf of the forest and stone of the mountains, in every shining star, in earth and sea and sky, God's name was written. With both the animate and the inanimate creation—with leaf and flower and tree, and with every living creature, from the leviathan of the waters to the mote in the sunbeam—the dwellers in Eden held converse, gathering from each the secrets of its life. God's glory in the heavens, the innumerable worlds in their orderly revolutions, 'the balancings of the clouds' (Job 37:16), the mysteries of light and sound, of day and night—all were objects of study by the pupils of earth's first school....

"As it came from the Creator's hand, not only the Garden of Eden but the whole earth was exceedingly beautiful. No taint of sin, or shadow of death, marred the fair creation. God's glory 'covered the heavens, and the earth was full of his praise.' 'The morning stars sang together, and all the sons of God shouted for joy.' Habakkuk 3:3; Job 38:7. Thus was the earth a fit emblem of Him who is 'abundant in goodness and truth' (Exodus 34:6); a fit study for those who were made in His image. The Garden of Eden was a representation of what God desired the whole earth to become, and it was His purpose that, as the human family increased in numbers, they should establish other homes and schools like the one He had given. Thus in course of time the whole earth might be occupied with homes and schools where the words and the works of God should be studied, and where the students should thus be fitted more and more fully to reflect, throughout endless ages, the light of the knowledge of His glory" (Ed 20-22, 1903).

"In the garden that God prepared as a home for His children, graceful shrubs and delicate flowers greeted the eye at every turn. There were trees of every variety, many of them laden with fragrant and delicious fruit. On their branches the birds caroled their songs of praise. Under their shadow the creatures of the earth sported together without a fear.

"Adam and Eve, in their untainted purity, delighted in the sights and sounds of Eden. God appointed them their work in the garden, 'to dress it and to keep it.' Genesis 2:15. Each day's labor brought them health and gladness, and the happy pair greeted with joy the visits of their Creator, as in the cool of the day He walked and talked with them. Daily God taught them His lessons" (MH 261, 1905).

> *"God gave to our first parents the means of true education when He instructed them to till the soil and care for their garden home."*

"God gave to our first parents the means of true education when He instructed them to till the soil and care for their garden home. After sin came in, through disobedience to the Lord's requirements, the work to be done in cultivating the ground was greatly multiplied; for the earth because of the curse, brought forth weeds and thistles. But the employment itself was not given because of sin. The great Master Himself blessed the work of tilling the soil" (Ms85-1908).

God's Plan for His Chosen People
"The education centering in the family was that which prevailed in the days of the patriarchs. For the schools thus established, God provided the conditions most favorable for the development of character. The people who were under His direction still pursued the plan of life that He had appointed in the beginning. Those who departed from God built for themselves cities, and, congregating in them, gloried in the splendor, the luxury, and the vice that make the cities of today the world's pride and its curse. But the men who held fast God's principles of life dwelt among the fields and hills. They were tillers of the soil and keepers of flocks and herds, and in this free, independent life, with its opportunities for labor and study and meditation, they learned of God and taught their children of His works and ways" (Ed 33, 1903).

"By the distribution of the land among the people, God provided for them, as for the dwellers in Eden, the occupation most favorable to development—the care of plants and animals. A further provision for education was the suspension of agricultural labor every seventh year, the land lying fallow, and its spontaneous products being left to the poor. Thus was given opportunity for more extended study, for social intercourse and worship, and for the exercise of benevolence, so often crowded out by life's cares and labors" (Ed 43, 1903).

"In God's plan for Israel every family had a home on the land, with sufficient ground for tilling. Thus were provided both the means and the incentive for a useful, industrious, and self-supporting life. And no devising of men has ever improved upon that plan. To the world's departure from it is owing, to a large degree, the poverty and wretchedness that exist today" (MH 183, 1905).

"The pupils of these schools [of the Prophets] sustained themselves by their own labor in tilling the soil or in some mechanical employment. In Israel this was not thought strange or degrading; indeed, it was regarded a crime to allow children to grow up in ignorance of useful labor. By the command of God every child was taught some trade, even though he was to be educated for holy office. Many of the religious teachers supported themselves by manual labor. Even so late as the time of the apostles, Paul and Aquila were no less honored because they earned a livelihood by their trade of tentmaking" (PP 593, 1890).

[Alternate version] "The pupils of these schools sustained themselves by their own labor in tilling the soil or in some mechanical employment. In Israel this was not thought strange or degrading; indeed, it was regarded as a sin to allow children to grow up in ignorance of useful labor. Every youth, whether his parents were rich or poor, was taught some trade. Even though he was to be educated for holy office, a knowledge of practical life was regarded as essential to the greatest usefulness. Many, also, of the teachers supported themselves by manual labor" (Ed 47, 1903).

"The Waldenses had sacrificed their worldly prosperity for the truth's sake, and with persevering patience they toiled for their bread. Every spot of tillable land among the mountains was carefully improved; the valleys and the less fertile hillsides were made to yield their increase. Economy and severe self-denial formed a part of the education which the children received as their only legacy. They were taught that God designs life to be a discipline, and that their wants could be supplied only by personal labor, by forethought, care, and faith. The process was laborious and wearisome, but it was wholesome, just what man needs in his fallen state, the school which God has provided for his training and development.

"While the youth were inured to toil and hardship, the culture of the intellect was not neglected. They were taught that all their powers belonged to God, and that all were to be improved and developed for his service" (4SP 73, 1884).

God's Plan for the New Earth
"In the earth made new, the redeemed will engage in the occupations and pleasures that brought happiness to Adam and Eve in the beginning. The Eden life will be lived, the life in garden and field. 'They shall build houses, and inhabit them; and they shall plant vineyards, and eat the fruit of them. They shall not build, and another inhabit; they shall not plant, and another eat: for as the days of a tree are the days of my people, and mine elect shall long enjoy the work of their hands.' Isaiah 65:21, 22" (PK 730, 1917).

Promises for the Agriculturalist

"The Lord expects us to work in order that we obtain food. He does not propose that we shall gather the harvest unless we break the sod, till the soil, and cultivate the produce. Then God sends the rain and the sunshine and the clouds to cause vegetation to flourish. God works and man cooperates with God. Then there is seed time and harvest" (Lt35-1890).

"The Lord gives the showers of rain and the blessed sunshine. He gives to men all their power; let them devote heart and mind and strength to doing His will in obedience to his commandments.... Let them ... commit themselves to God, working with their endowment of physical strength, and their labor will not be in vain. That God who has made the world for the benefit of man will provide means from the earth to sustain the diligent worker. The seed placed in thoroughly prepared soil, will produce its harvest. God can spread a table for his people in the wilderness....

"The earth has its concealed treasures, and the Lord would have thousands and tens of thousands working upon the soil who are crowded into the cities to watch for a chance to earn a trifle....

"The earth is to be made to give forth its strength, but without the blessing of God it can do nothing. In the beginning, God looked upon all he had made, and pronounced it very good. The curse was brought upon the earth in consequence of sin, but shall this curse be multiplied by increasing sin? Ignorance is doing its baleful work. Slothful servants are increasing the evil by their lazy habits. Many are unwilling to earn their bread by the sweat of their brow, and they refuse to till the soil. But the earth has blessings hidden in her depths for those who have the courage and will and perseverance to gather her treasures....

"False witness has been borne in condemning land which, if properly worked, would yield rich returns. The narrow plans, the little strength put forth, the little study as to the best methods, call loudly for reform. The people need to learn that patient labor will do wonders" (Ms8a-1894).

"God does not work miracles where he has provided means by which the work may be accomplished. Use your time and talents in his service, and he will not fail to work with your efforts. If the farmer fails to plow and sow, God does not work a miracle to undo the results of his neglect. Harvest-time finds his fields barren—there are no sheaves to be reaped, no grain to be garnered. God provided the seed and the soil, the sun and the rain; and if the agriculturist had employed the means that were at his hand, he would have received according to his sowing and his labor" (CE 116, 1894).

> *"If, with the word of God in your heart, you go forth to... cultivate the soil, you will find your hearts softened and subdued by the Holy Spirit."*

"How much the student of nature can learn of God if, at the same time, he will become a student of the word! If, with the word of God in your heart, you go forth to break up and cultivate the soil, you will find your hearts softened and subdued by the Holy Spirit of God. The mind will be opened to the teachings of God in the natural world" (YI June 30, 1898).

"Through disobedience to God, Adam and Eve had lost Eden, and because of sin the whole earth was cursed. But if God's people followed His instruction, their land would be restored to fertility and beauty. God Himself gave them directions in regard to the culture of the soil, and they were to co-operate with Him in its restoration. Thus the whole land, under God's control, would become an object lesson of spiritual truth. As in obedience to His natural laws the earth should produce its treasures, so in obedience to His moral law the hearts of the people were to reflect the attributes of His character. Even the heathen would recognize the superiority of those who served and worshiped the living God" (COL 289, 1900).

"If the land is cultivated, it will, with the blessing of God, supply our necessities. We are not to be discouraged about temporal things because of apparent failures, nor should we be disheartened by delay. We should work the soil cheerfully, hopefully, gratefully, believing that the earth holds in her bosom rich stores for the faithful worker to garner, stores richer than gold or silver. The niggardliness laid to her charge is false witness. With proper, intelligent cultivation the earth will yield its treasures for the benefit of man. The mountains and hills are changing; the earth is waxing old like a garment; but the blessing of God, which spreads a table for His people in the wilderness, will never cease" (6T 178, 1901).

"He who taught Adam and Eve in Eden how to tend the garden, desires to instruct men today. There is wisdom for him who drives the plow and sows the seed. Before those who trust and obey Him, God will open ways of advance. Let them move forward courageously, trusting in Him to supply their needs according to the riches of His goodness" (MH 200, 1905).

"The Lord has given the sunshine and the rain, and has caused the fruit to grow, and the earth to produce that which may be prepared for the food of mankind. He requires His family diligently to till the soil, that it may produce those things that may be used as food. They are to plant the seed, and care for it as it grows. This is the provision that He has made for man's food. He has given genius and tact to man, that he may prepare from the fruit of the earth a great variety of foods. Grains, vegetables, and fruits are to be planted and cultivated. The ground is to be dressed and worked, and the earth will produce her treasures" (Lt354-1906).

"We each have a work to do for God, whatever may be our occupation. Those who are on their farms are not to think that it would be a waste of time for them to plan to go out and visit their neighbors, and hold up before them the light of the truth for this time; for even if it does seem difficult to leave the farm work, yet we shall not lose financially because of spending time in helping others. There is a God in heaven that will bless our labors" (Ms15-1909).

"You are not working alone. When you are tempted to become discouraged, remember this: Angels of God are right around you. They will minister to the very ground and the earth, causing it to give forth its treasures" (Ms13-1909).

A Call for Christian Farmers

"To many of those living in the cities who have not a spot of green grass to set their feet upon, who year after year have looked out upon filthy courts and narrow alleys, brick walls and pavements, and skies clouded with dust and smoke—if these could be taken to some farming district, surrounded with the green fields, the woods and hills and brooks, the clear skies and the fresh, pure air of the country, it would seem almost like heaven.

"Cut off to a great degree from contact with and dependence upon men, and separated from the world's corrupting maxims and customs and excitements, they would come nearer to the heart of nature. God's presence would be more real to them. Many would learn the lesson of dependence upon Him. Through nature they would hear His voice speaking to their hearts of His peace and love, and mind and soul and body would respond to the healing, life-giving power.

"If they ever become industrious and self-supporting, very many must have assistance, encouragement, and instruction. There are multitudes of poor families for whom no better missionary work could be done than to assist them in settling on the land and in learning how to make it yield them a livelihood.

"The need for such help and instruction is not confined to the cities. Even in the country, with all its possibilities for a better life, multitudes of the poor are in great need. Whole communities are devoid of education in industrial and sanitary lines. Families live in hovels, with scant furniture and clothing, without tools, without books, destitute both of comforts and conveniences and of means of culture. Imbruted souls, bodies weak and ill-formed, reveal the results of evil heredity and of wrong habits. These people must be educated from the very foundation. They have led shiftless, idle, corrupt lives, and they need to be trained to correct habits.

"How can they be awakened to the necessity of improvement? How can they be directed to a higher ideal of life? How can they be helped to rise? What can be done where poverty prevails and is to be contended with at every step? Certainly the work is difficult. The necessary reformation will never be made unless men and women are assisted by a power outside of themselves. It is God's purpose that the rich and the poor shall be closely bound together by the ties of sympathy and helpfulness. Those who have means, talents, and capabilities are to use these gifts in blessing their fellow men.

"Christian farmers can do real missionary work in helping the poor to find homes on the land and in teaching them how to till the soil and make it productive. Teach them how to use the implements of agriculture, how to cultivate various crops, how to plant and care for orchards.

"Many who till the soil fail to secure adequate returns because of their neglect. Their orchards are not properly cared for, the crops are not put in at the right time, and a mere surface work is done in cultivating the soil. Their ill success they charge to the unproductiveness of the land. False witness is often borne in condemning land that, if properly worked, would yield rich returns. The narrow plans, the little strength put forth, the little study as to the best methods, call loudly for reform.

"Let proper methods be taught to all who are willing to learn. If any do not wish you to speak to them of advanced ideas, let the lessons be given silently. Keep up the culture of your own land. Drop a word to your neighbors when you can, and let the harvest be eloquent in favor of right methods. Demonstrate what can be done with the land when properly worked" (MH 191–193, 1905).

"We saw large tracts of land used only for grazing cattle and sheep. We were surprised to see these lands unimproved by cultivation. We thought of some of our American brethren who were industrious and economical (who understand agriculture). Had these lands [been] in their possession, with their knowledge of agriculture, what a change would be wrought in this place, Gisborne [New Zealand]. There would be earnest work to uproot the sweetbriers which were growing so abundantly in these beautiful grounds, and in their place would be cultivated lands, orchards, and abundance of vegetables and small fruits.

"Occasionally we would see an orchard. Fruit trees do well. The peach, the lemon trees, and apples, quinces, plums, and cherries, but the orchards are so few and small. When I considered what might be done in this place if some of the industry, tact, and wise planning of some in America could have the handling of this land, I wanted to speak to you over the broad Pacific and say to some who could come to this beautiful place, 'Come and show what your agricultural knowledge and practice will reveal in this place.'...

"The five weeks' stay in this place is about ended, and I have the explanation of why the land is largely left unimproved except for the grazing of cattle. It is the many holidays which [are] following one upon another in rapid succession that is leaving the lands uncultivated" (Ms101-1893).

The Australian Field

"I think no better missionary work could be done than to settle poor families on the land. Every family shall sign a contract that they will work the land according to the plans specified. Someone must be appointed to direct the working of the land, and under his supervision orange trees, and fruit trees of every appropriate description should be planted. Peach orchards would yield quick return. Vegetable gardens would bring forth good crops. This must be done at once. We have some six weeks yet to set things in running order, and with God's blessing on the land, we shall see what it will produce.

"The question was asked of Moses, Can the Lord spread a table in the wilderness? The question may be asked, Will this land at Dora Creek produce as abundantly as Sister White believes that it will? Time will tell. We must test the matter before we can speak assuredly, but we are willing to risk much, provided we can place the supervision of this enterprise under an understanding America farmer. We do want to demonstrate what will be done with the land when it is properly worked. When once this is done, we shall be able to help the poor who live in Australia in a far better way than by giving them money as we have had to do in the past" (Lt29-1894).

"The people need to be educated as to how to raise fruit and grains. If we had several experienced farmers who would come to this country and work up the land and demonstrate what the land would yield, they would be doing grand missionary work for the people.... They [local farmers] think that what has been done must be done. Their ideas are stereotyped. We intend to cultivate land, and show them how it can be done....

"If some of our intelligent American farmers would educate the people so that they could work their land and bring produce into the market for home consumption, and for regions beyond, so that money might be brought back into the country, they would do a good missionary work. They would find work for thousands that are crowding into our large cities, seeking office work or trying to pick up a few odd jobs, that would barely enable them to exist" (Lt89a-1894).

"There is science in the humblest kind of work, and if all would thus regard it, they would see nobility in labor. Heart and soul are to be put into work of any kind; then there is cheerfulness and efficiency. In agricultural and mechanical occupations men may give evidence to God that they appreciate His gift in the physical powers, and the mental faculties as well. Let the educated ability be employed in devising improved methods of work. This is just what the Lord wants. There is honor in any class of work that is essential to be done....

"Men are needed in different communities to show the people how riches are to be obtained from the soil. The cultivations of land will bring its return....

> *"Men are needed in different communities to show the people how riches are to be obtained from the soil."*

"Men take you to their orchards of oranges and lemons and other fruits, and tell you that the produce does not pay for the work done in them. It is next to impossible to make ends meet, and parents decide that [the] children shall not be farmers; they have not the courage and hope to educate them to till the soil.

"What is needed is schools to educate and train the youth so that they will know how to overcome this condition of things. There must be education in the sciences, and education in plans and methods of working the soil. There is hope in the soil, but brain and heart and strength must be brought into the work of tilling it. The money devoted to horse racing, theater going, gambling, and lotteries, the money spent in the public houses for beer and strong drink—let it be expended in making the land productive, and we shall see a different state of things.

"This country needs educated farmers. The Lord gives the showers of rain and the blessed sunshine. He gives to men all their powers; let them devote heart and mind and strength to doing His will in obedience to His commandments. Let them cut off every pernicious habit, never expending a penny for beer or liquor of any kind, nor for tobacco, having nothing to do with horse racing or similar sports, then commit themselves to God, working with their endowment of physical strength, and their labor will not be in vain. That God who has made the world for the benefit of man will provide means from the earth to sustain the diligent worker. The seed placed in thoroughly prepared soil will produce its harvest. God can spread a table for his people in the wilderness....

"There is [a] great want of intelligent men to till the soil, who will be thorough. This knowledge will not be a hindrance to the education essential for business or for usefulness in any line. To develop the capacity of the soil requires thought and intelligence. Not only will it develop muscle, but capability for study, because the taxation of brain and muscle is equalized. We should so train the youth that they will love to work upon the land, and delight in improving it. The hope of advancing the cause of God in this country is in creating a new moral taste in love of work, which will transform mind and character.

"False witness has been borne in condemning land which, if properly worked, would yield rich returns. The narrow plans, the little strength put forth, the little study as to the best methods, call loudly for reform. The people need to learn that patient labor will do wonders. There is much mourning over unproductive soil, when if men would read the Old Testament Scriptures they would see that the Lord knew much better than they in regard to the proper treatment of land. After being cultivated for several years, and giving her treasure to the possession of man, portions of the land should be allowed to rest, and then the crops should be changed....

"Let God's glory be kept ever in view; and if the crop is a failure, be not discouraged; try again; but remember that you can have no harvest unless the ground is properly prepared for the seed; failure may be wholly due to neglect on this point....

"God would be glorified if men from other countries who have acquired an intelligent knowledge of agriculture, would come to this land, and by precept and example teach the people how to cultivate the soil, that it may yield rich treasures. Men are wanted to educate others how to plow, and how to use the implements of agriculture. Who will be missionaries to do this work, to teach proper methods to the youth, and to all who feel willing and humble enough to learn? If any do not want you to give them improved ideas, let the lessons be given by silently showing what can be done in setting out orchards and planting corn; let the harvest be eloquent in favor of right methods of labor. Drop a word to your neighbors when you can, keep up the culture of your own land, and that will educate....

"Farmers need far more intelligence in their work. In most cases it is their own fault if they do not see the land yielding its harvest. They should be constantly learning how to secure a variety of treasures from the earth. The people should learn as far as possible to depend upon the products that they can obtain from the soil. In every phase of this kind of labor they can be educating the mind to work for the saving of souls for whom Christ has died. 'Ye are God's husbandry; ye are God's building....'

"He who taught Adam and Eve in Eden how to tend the garden, would instruct men today. There is wisdom for him who holds the plow, and plants and sows the seed. The earth has its concealed treasures, and the Lord would have thousands and tens of thousands working upon the soil who are crowded into the cities to watch for a chance to earn a trifle....

"The earth is to be made to give forth its strength; but without the blessing of God it could do nothing. In the beginning, God looked upon all that He had made, and pronounced it very good. The curse was brought upon the earth in consequence of sin. But shall this curse be multiplied by increasing sin? Ignorance is doing its baleful work. Slothful servants are increasing the evil by their lazy habits. Many are unwilling to earn their bread by the sweat of their brow, and they refuse to till the soil. But the earth has blessings hidden in her depths for those who have courage and will and perseverance to gather her treasures....

"Many farmers have failed to secure adequate returns from their land because they have undertaken the work as though it was a degrading employment; they do not see that there is a blessing in it for themselves and their families. All they can discern is the brand of servitude. Their orchards are neglected, the crops are not put in at the right season, and a mere surface work is done in cultivating the soil. Many neglect their farms in order to keep holidays and to attend horse races and betting clubs; their money is expended in shows and lotteries and idleness, and then they plead that they cannot obtain money to cultivate the soil and improve their farms; but had they more money, the result would still be the same" (Ms8a-1894).

"We should judge that the general difficulty with farming here is a lack of interest. There is plenty of idleness, numerous holidays which are improved in following many kinds of objectionable amusements.... But if the soil was cultivated, it would produce excellent fruit. Because of the slack, slipshod way the landholders cultivate their farms, nothing flourishes as it should, and the impression made upon those who view the land is that it is too poor to yield a good crop.

"I have been anxious that the land should be taken in hand and thoroughly worked. Even the orange trees are left to grow up amid the grass as wild trees grow. But where such immense trees flourish as flourish here, many of them growing up perfectly straight toward heaven, I am convinced that with the blessing of God, with diligence and faithfulness in working the land, farmers might produce gratifying results, and in return for the labor put forth they might reap a good harvest. I have thought of the many families who are crowded in our large cities, and I have thought how pleased I would be if some of them would come to this place and put forth their energies in clearing the land, and in subduing and cultivating the soil....

"We examined the way in which they work the land, and found that the plough had been put in only to about the depth of six inches. An intelligent American farmer would not regard this as a faithful way of working the land. Those who work in this cheap, superficial way cannot expect to receive anything out of harmony with their method, but in accordance with it....

"The more I see the school property the more I am amazed at the cheap price at which it has been purchased. When the board wants to go back on this purchase, I pledge myself to secure the land. I will settle it with poor families; I will have missionary families come out from America and do the best kind of missionary work in educating the people as to how to till the soil and make it productive. I have planned what can be raised in different places. I have said, 'Here can be alfalfa, there can be strawberries, here can be sweet corn and common corn, and this ground will raise good potatoes, while that will raise good fruit of all kinds.' So in imagination I have all the different places in flourishing condition" (Ms35-1894).

"There will be [a] new presentation of men as bread winners, possessing educated, trained ability to work the soil to advantage. Their minds will not be overtaxed and strained to the uttermost with a study of the sciences. Such men will break down the foolish sentiments that have prevailed in regard to manual labor. An influence will go forth, not in loud-voiced oratory, but in real inculcation of ideas. We shall see farmers who are not coarse and rough and slack, careless of their apparel and of the appearance of their homes; but they will bring taste into farmhouses.... The cultivation of the soil will be regarded as elevating and ennobling.

Pure, practical religion will be manifested in treating the earth as God's treasurehouse. The more intelligent a man becomes, the more religious influence should be radiating from him. And the Lord would have us treat the earth as a precious treasure, lent us in trust" (Lt47a-1895).

"Fathers should train their sons to engage with them in their trades and employments. Farmers should not think that agriculture is a business that is not elevated enough for their sons. Agriculture should be advanced by scientific knowledge. Farming has been pronounced unprofitable. People say that the soil does not pay for the labor expended upon it, and they bemoan the hard fate of those who till the soil. In this country [Australia] many have given up the idea that the land will pay for working it, and thousands of acres lie unimproved. But should persons of proper ability take hold of this line of employment, and make a study of the soil, and learn how to plant, to cultivate, and to gather in the harvest, more encouraging results might be seen. Many say, 'We have tried agriculture, and know what its results are,' and yet these very ones need to know how to cultivate the soil, and to bring science into their work. Their plowshares should cut deeper, broader furrows, and they need to learn that in tilling the soil they need not become common and coarse in their natures. Let them learn to bring religion into their work. Let them learn to put in the seed in its season, to give attention to vegetation, and to follow the plan that God has devised.

"The farmer and his sons have the open book of nature before them, and they should learn that farming is a noble occupation, when the work is done in a proper manner. The opinion that prevails that farming degrades the man, is erroneous. The earth is God's own creation, and he calls it very good. The hands may become hard and rough, but this hardness need not extend to the soul. The heart need not become careless, nor the soul defiled. The effeminate paleness may be tanned from the countenance, but the testimony of health is seen in the red and brown of the complexion. Christlikeness may be preserved in the farmer's life. Men may learn, in cultivating the soil, precious lessons about the cultivation of the Spirit" (ST August 13, 1896).

> *"Farming is a noble occupation, when the work is done in a proper manner."*

"The Lord would have all who are in His service to be learners. The tillers of the soil, the mechanics, the men who have learned their trades, are still to be learning better methods, expanding, enlarging in their ideas. Those who do not think they can learn anything are not the ones who can be a blessing in the enterprises in which we are engaged. Those who are willing to learn are wanted. God is continually leading and instructing" (BEcho August 24, 1896).

"God said to Adam, and to all the descendants of Adam, In the sweat of thy face shalt thou eat bread; for from henceforth the earth must be worked under the drawback of transgression. Thorns and briars shall it produce.

"In the parable of the wheat and tares, the servant is represented as saying to the husbandman, Didst not thou sow good seed in thy field? How then hath it tares? Did the husbandman sow the tares? No; he answered, 'An enemy hath done this.' The enemy always sows the tares. Neither God nor His angels ever dropped a seed that would produce a tare. The enemy of God and man does this evil work, in order to afflict the human family. By making labor tenfold harder, so that much exertion is required for the cultivation of the earth, Satan leads men to murmur against the God of heaven as the cause of their misery. But Satan is the real cause of it. He makes labor toilsome, and by indulging do-nothing habits, men co-operate with him. By their own neglect, they bring about such a condition of things that briars and thorns multiply and choke the good seed.

"Many desire to acquire means and be prosperous without perseveringly exercising brain, bone, and muscle. This course often destroys the motive required for efficiency. Their object is not gained, and they complain and murmur against God because the earth does not yield its increase as they expected it. But in nine cases out of ten, the failure of the harvest is the result of the slack efforts of the workers. They did not work with persevering energy at the right time. They did not prepare for the harvest by preparing and enriching the soil. They worked by impulse.

"The soil needs thoughtful attention. It must be plowed often and deep with a view to keeping out the weeds, which take nourishment from the good seed planted. Thus those who plough and sow prepare for the harvest. None need to stand in the field amid the sad wreck of their hopes" (Ms84-1897).

"Mr. H. C. Thompson, our farmer, then presented some of the products of the soil. Oranges and lemons from our school orchard, sweet potatoes and other products from the garden, were shown with pride; for they were all of extraordinary size and quality. He spoke briefly of what may be realized as the result of a faithful cultivation of the land, and pointed out that some of the difficulties that must be encountered by the agriculturist in this climate are largely compensated for by the fact that we can successfully engage in the cultivation of garden crops all the year around.

"The meeting closed with an earnest appeal from the chairman for the people of Cooranbong and vicinity to unite in the development of the district by the planting of orchards and the cultivation of garden produce, so that all may live upon the products of the soil, and not have to subsist on the bodies of dead animals.

"The good influence of this meeting was felt throughout the week of prayer; and the spirit of cordial friendship continues to grow" (RH October 11, 1898).

"I have been broken off to have a talk with Brother Martin. I furnish him papers and tracts to do missionary work. He is not a minister, but a farmer of considerable intelligence. He sells fruit, and thus becomes acquainted with the people. Many souls have been converted through his zealous influence" (Lt43-1899).

The Southern (U.S.) Field

"Why should not Seventh-day Adventists become true laborers together with God in seeking to save the souls of the colored race? Why should not many, instead of a few, go forth to labor in this long neglected field? Where are the families who will become missionaries, and who will engage in labor in this field? Where are the men who have means and experience so that they can go forth to these people and work for them just where they are?

"There are men who can educate them in agricultural lines, who can teach the colored people to sow seed and plant orchards. There are others who can teach them to read, and can give them an object lesson from their own life and example. Show them what you yourself can do to gain a livelihood, and it will be an education to them. Are we not called upon to do this very work? Are there not many who need to learn to love God supremely and their fellow men as themselves? In the Southern field are thousands of people who have souls to save or to lose. Are there not many among those who claim to believe the truth who will go forth into this field to do the work for which Christ gave up His ease, His riches, and His life?" (Ms21a-1895).

"In His providence, God is saying, as He has been saying for years past: Here is a field for you to work. Those who are wise in agricultural lines, in tilling the soil, those who can construct simple, plain buildings, may help.

They can do good work and at the same time show in their characters the high morality which it is the privilege of this people to attain to. Teach them the truth in simple object lessons. Make everything upon which they lay their hands a lesson in character building" (Ms164-1897).

[Alternate version] "Those who are wise in agricultural lines, in tilling the soil, those who can construct simple, plain buildings, may help. They can do good work and at the same time show in their characters the high standard to which it is the privilege of this people to attain. Let farmers, financiers, builders, and those who are skilled in various other crafts, go to neglected fields, to improve the land, to establish industries, to prepare humble homes for themselves, and to give their neighbors a knowledge of the truth for this time" (9T 36, 1909).

"There is to be a work done in the South, and it needs men and women who will not need to be preachers so much as teachers—humble men who are not afraid to work as farmers to educate the Southerners how to till the soil, for whites and blacks need to be educated in this line" (Lt102a, 1899).

Cautions to Farmers

> *"Let not the care and perplexity of farms here engross your mind, but you can safely be wrapped up in contemplating Abraham's farm."*

"Let not the care and perplexity of farms here engross your mind, but you can safely be wrapped up in contemplating Abraham's farm. We are heirs to that immortal inheritance. Wean your affections from earth, and dwell upon heavenly things" (1T 118, 1868).

"Dear Brother E, you have made a great mistake in giving this world your ambition. You are exacting and sometimes impatient, and at times require too much of your son. He has become discouraged. At your house it has been work, work, work, from early morning until night. Your large farm has brought extra cares and burdens into your house. You have talked upon business; for business was primary in your mind, and 'out of the abundance of the heart the mouth speaketh.' Has your example in your family exalted Christ and His salvation above your farming interest and your desire for gain? If your children fail of everlasting life, the blood of their souls will surely be found on the garments of their father" (4T 48, 1881).

"Men act as though they were bereft of their reason. They are buried up in the cares of this life. They have no time to devote to God, no time to serve him. Work, work, work, is the order of the day. All about them are required to go upon the high-pressure plan, to take care of large farms. To tear down and build greater is their ambition, that they may have room wherein to bestow their goods. Yet these very men who are weighed down with their riches, pass for Christ's followers. They have the name of believing that Christ is soon to come, that the end of all things is at hand; yet they have no spirit of sacrifice. They are plunging deeper and deeper into the world. They allow themselves but little time to study the word of life, and to meditate and pray. Neither do they give others in their family, or those who serve them, this privilege. Yet these men profess to believe that this world is not their home—that they are merely pilgrims and strangers upon the earth, preparing to move to a better country. The example and influence of all such is a curse to the cause of God. Hollow hypocrisy characterizes their professed Christian life. They love God and the truth just as much as their works show, and no more. A man will act out all the faith he has. 'By their fruits ye shall know them.' The heart is where the treasure is. Their treasure is upon this earth, and their heart and interests are here' (RH February 23, 1886).

"But farmers themselves must get educated to give heed to the laws of life and health by regulating their labor, even if there is some loss in their grain or the harvesting of crops. Farmers work too hard and too constantly, and violate the laws of God in their physical nature. This is the worst kind of economy. For a day he may accomplish more, yet in the end he is a loser by his ill management of himself" (Lt85-1888).

"Instead of rendering to God the means He has placed in their hands, many invest it in more land. This evil is growing with our brethren. They had before all they could well care for, but the love of money or a desire to be counted as well off as their neighbors leads them to bury their means in the world and withhold from God His just dues. Can we be surprised if they are not prospered? if God does not bless their crops and they are disappointed? Could our brethren remember that God can bless twenty acres of land and make them as productive as one hundred, they would not continue to bury themselves in lands, but would let their means flow into God's treasury. 'Take heed,' said Christ, 'lest at any time your hearts be overcharged with surfeiting, and drunkenness, and cares of this life.' Satan is pleased to have you increase your farms and invest your means in worldly enterprises, for by so doing you not only hinder the cause from advancing, but by anxiety and overwork lessen your prospect for eternal life" (5T 151, 1889).

"The farmer can tell you about his farm, he can describe the quality of the land, and the character of its products. He can speak of what he knows with great freedom and interest. The lawyer, the merchant, the mechanic, all prepare for their pursuits, and experience makes perfect their knowledge, and they can all talk easily and earnestly of the improvements made in their calling; but bring together all those workmen who profess religion in such a meeting as this, and many will speak of their faith with hesitancy, with stammering tongue, and in so low a tone of voice that it is difficult to understand what they say. Why is it that men and women who can speak intelligently about matters of temporal interest, cannot speak decidedly about things of eternal interest? How do the angels look upon our lack of appreciation of the things of God? Why is it that there is such a deficiency in the service we profess to render to God?" (ST May 13, 1889).

"The wealthy farmers are some of them acting as if in the day of God the Lord only would require of them to present to him enriched, improved farms, building added to building, and they say, 'Here, Lord, are thy talents; behold, I have gained all this possession.' If the acres of their farms were so many precious souls saved to Jesus Christ, if their buildings were so many souls to be presented to the Master, then he could say to these men, 'Well done, good and faithful servant.' But you cannot take these improved farms, or these buildings, into heaven. The fires of the last days will consume them. If you invest and bury your talents of means in these earthly treasures, your heart is on them, your anxiety is for them, your persevering labor is for them, your tact, your skill is cultivated to serve earthly, worldly possessions, and is not directed or employed upon heavenly things" (ST Feb. 8, 1892).

"May the Lord bless you abundantly, my brother, in your home. The charge I have to give you is: Do not load yourself down with so many burdens that you will fail to do your duty to your children. I do not write these words as a reproach, but as a reminder. If anything must be neglected, let it be the care of inanimate things. Keep your own soul fresh and pure and uplifted. If you give your children the attention they need, some things may have to be neglected. Then let them be. Your children are building characters for time and for eternity, and you must make no mistakes in dealing with them. Be assured that I will not censure you for anything left undone on the farm.

"May the peace of God abide in your home. May His blessing rest upon your little flock. They are lambs of His fold, and must be nurtured and cherished. Do not overwork. Do not strain every nerve and muscle to try to do everything that there is to do on the farm, but get help.

"May the Lord abundantly bless you and your wife and children" (Lt159-1904).

"Watch in your family. Don't speak a cross word. Don't raise the ire of your children when you should not, because this will not reform them. Take them aside and converse with them and pray with them, and read the Scriptures to them. What a work is this! This is what you want to do. Take time for it. You may say, My farm. Yes, but cannot God bless your farm better if you have a united family, to speak the same things, to work the same order? And will not the Lord let His rich grace rest upon you in wisdom and righteousness? (Ms111-1909).

Agriculture at Home

"To the parents of these children [who are practicing 'secret vice'] I would say, you have brought children into the world which are only a curse to society. Your children are unruly, passionate, quarrelsome, and vicious. Their influence upon others is corrupting. These children bear the stamp of the baser passions of the father. The stamp of his character is placed upon his children. His hasty, violent temper is reflected in his children. These parents should have long ago removed to the country, separating themselves and children from the society of those they could not benefit, but only harm.

"Steady industry upon a farm would have proved a blessing to these children, and constant employment, as their strength could bear, would have given them less opportunity to corrupt their own bodies by self-abuse [masturbation], and would have prevented them from instructing a large number in this hellish practice. Labor is a great blessing to all children, especially to that class whose minds are naturally inclined to vice and depravity" (PH085, 1869).

"Every family should have a plat of ground for cultivation and for beauty. Parents, a flower garden will be a blessing to your children. Your daughters would have better health in working a portion of each day upon the shrubs and flowers, than the delicate employment of embroidery and crochet, which confines them in doors. Your children need active exercise in order to be healthful and happy.

"Parents, it will pay to expend a small sum yearly in purchasing flower seeds and shrubs. We have purchased these of James Vick, Rochester, N.Y., and have ever felt more than satisfied with the means we thus invested. You should help your children to arrange their gardens tastefully, and then assist them in planting their seeds and shrubs. Fathers should take an interest in these things for the benefit of their children, if they themselves have not a natural love for them.

"My husband takes as great a pleasure in my flower garden as myself and my children do. Frequently, when he has had hired help, has he left his labor, and set all hands to work in preparing my plat of ground in order for my plants and seeds. This manifest kindness and interest have encouraged a love for flowers and plants in the minds of our children, and many hours have they devoted to the pleasurable exercise of the cultivation of these flowers, which they might have spent in exciting amusements and in questionable society.

"We can all take pleasure in beholding the many beautiful varieties of opening buds, and blossoming flowers, of every description and hue, which our Heavenly Father has created for the happiness and benefit of his children.

"It is God's design that we should love the beautiful in nature. He made a garden for our first parents, and there planted with his own divine hand the trees for usefulness and ornament, and the beautiful vines bearing fruit, and the lovely flowers of every variety and color. This was for the pleasure and happiness of man. If parents would more closely follow the example of their Creator in this respect, I believe they would have less trouble in bringing up their children to usefulness and happiness. If parents would encourage their children to love the beauties of nature, they would throw about them a safeguard to preserve them from iniquity prevailing among the youth....

"By making home and its surroundings attractive, they will lessen the desire for exciting pleasures and amusements which are injurious to the physical, mental, and moral health of children. You can beautify your homes with fruit trees, and shrubs, and flowers, and encourage in the minds of your children a love for these things. You can teach them in relation to the better life, by connecting the beauties of nature, so marred, and imperfect, and short-lived, with the never-fading and immortal beauties of Eden restored. You can unite with nature's your lessons of the love and mercy of our beneficent Creator, who has given them all these things for their happiness. You should seek to draw their hearts from nature up to nature's God, and connect the mercy of God with the morning light, and the glories of the setting sun. His mercy is seen in the musical, murmuring streams, and even in frowning storms. Direct their minds to the mercy of God in the summer's heat and winter's cold. We can trace before them the mercy and wisdom of God in the falling of the blessed rain to refresh and enliven the parched earth and vegetation, and direct them to a love and wisdom that is infinite. Young hearts will respond to such lessons as these, and parents will be blessed in seeing the fruit of their labor in the physical, mental, and moral improvement of their loved ones" (HR March 1, 1871).

"The average father wastes many golden opportunities to attract and bind his children to him. Upon returning home from his business he should find it a pleasant change to spend some time with his children. He may take them into the garden, and show them the opening buds, and the varied tints of the blooming flowers. Through such mediums he may give them the most important lessons concerning the Creator, by opening before them the great book of nature, where the love of God is expressed in every tree, and flower, and blade of grass. He may impress upon their minds the fact that if God cares so much for the trees and flowers, he will care much more for the creatures formed in his image. He may lead them early to understand that God wants children to be lovely, not with artificial adornment, but with beauty of character, the charms of kindness and affection, which will make their hearts bound with joy and happiness" (HR September 1, 1877).

"To live in the country would be very beneficial to them [children of a single mother who was preoccupied with the cares of the world]; an active, out-of-door life would develop health of both mind and body. They should have a garden to cultivate, where they might find both amusement and useful employment. The training of plants and flowers tends to the improvement of taste and judgment, while an acquaintance with God's useful and beautiful creations has a refining and ennobling influence upon the mind, referring it to the Maker and Master of all" (4T 136, 1881).

> *"The training of plants and flowers tends to the improvement of taste and judgment."*

"Many parents remove from their country homes to the city, regarding it as a more desirable or profitable location. But by making this change they expose their children to many and great temptations. The boys have no employment, and they obtain a street education, and go on from one step in depravity to another, until they lose all interest in anything that is good and pure and holy. How much better had the parents remained with their families in the country, where the influences are most favorable for physical and mental strength. Let the youth be taught to labor in tilling the soil, and let them sleep the sweet sleep of weariness and innocence" (RH September 13, 1881).

"Let the mother take her children with her into the field or garden and from the things of nature draw lessons that will point them to nature's God, and aid them in the struggle against evil. Let her point them to the lofty trees, the shrubs, and the carpet of green that covers the earth. Let her teach them how the lily, striking its roots down deep through the mire into the sand below, gains nourishment that enables it to send up a pure, beautiful blossom. Then let her show them how, by rejecting that which is impure, and choosing that which is pure, they may grow up into pure, noble men and women" (Ms29-1886).

"Mothers, you should begin to discipline your child when it is a babe in your arms. Through childhood to youth, through youth to manhood, you should train your children for the family above. God does not desire you to take up your time in adorning your garments and decorating your homes, to the neglect of the education of your children. You should take your children out into the gardens, and show them the beautiful flowers that God has made. God is the great master artist, and the pictures which are painted by human artists and admired by the world, are only feeble imitations of the works of God. God daily works miracles before us in the unfolding of the blossoms; for no human hand can paint such delicate hues, or fashion such graceful plants. All this speaks of the work of the divine Artist, and each flower is an expression of the love of God to us. God has designed to make us happy. He has covered the earth with the beautiful green verdure; for he knew that this color would be grateful to our senses. Each beautiful thing in nature is a token of God's love and care. So take your children out into the open air beneath the canopy of the heavens, under the noble trees, into the gardens, and point them through nature up to nature's God. Carry their minds up to contemplate the works of God in nature that they may learn to love him in their childhood and youth. Do not weary them with long prayers and tedious exhortations, but teach them to be obedient to the law of God. Teach them to be kind and courteous, tell them that if they are rude and unlovely in disposition, they cannot enter into the kingdom of heaven where all is peace and love. We are here to be trained for the family above" (RH February 23, 1892).

"Those who will take their families into the country, place them where they have fewer temptations. The children who are with parents that love and fear God, are in every way much better situated to learn of the Great Teacher, who is the source and fountain of wisdom. They have a much more favorable opportunity to gain a fitness for the kingdom of heaven. Send the children to schools located in the city, where every phase of temptation is waiting to attract and demoralize them, and the work of character building is tenfold harder for both parents and children....

> *"Fathers and mothers who possess a piece of land and a comfortable home are kings and queens."*

"Fathers and mothers who possess a piece of land and a comfortable home are kings and queens" (Ms8a-1894).

"Do not send your little ones away to school too early. The mother should be careful how she trusts the moulding of the infant mind to other hands. Parents ought to be the best teachers of their children until they have reached eight or ten years of age. Their schoolroom should be the open air, amid the flowers and birds, and their text-book the treasure of nature. As fast as their minds can comprehend it, the parents should open before them God's great book of nature. These lessons, given amid such surroundings, will not soon be forgotten. Great pains should be taken to prepare the souls of the heart for the Sower to scatter the good seed. If half the time and labor that is now worse than wasted in following the fashions of the world, were devoted to the cultivation of the minds of the children, to the formation of correct habits, a marked change would be apparent in families" (CE 170, 1894).

"How many go out into the garden with their children, and as they point them to the beautiful flowers say, 'This is an expression of the love of God to you'? This would lead their minds up through nature to nature's God. Would not this be far more profitable to your children than taking them to all the shows and amusements of a demoralizing nature that would absorb their attention so that they forget God?" (BEcho November 19, 1894).

"Fathers and mothers, let your children learn from the flowers. Take them with you into garden and field and under the leafy trees, and teach them to read in nature the message of God's love. Let the thoughts of Him be linked with bird and flower and tree. Lead the children to see in every pleasant and beautiful thing an expression of God's love for them. Recommend your religion to them by its pleasantness. Let the law of kindness be in your lips.

"Teach the children that because of God's great love their natures may be changed and brought into harmony with His. Teach them that He would have their lives beautiful with the graces of the flowers. Teach them, as they gather the sweet blossoms, that He who made the flowers is more beautiful than they. Thus the tendrils of their hearts will be entwined about Him. He who is 'altogether lovely' will become to them as a daily companion and familiar friend, and their lives will be transformed into the image of His purity" (MB 97, 98, 1896).

"Education means more than the mere studying of books. It is necessary that both the physical and mental powers be exercised in order to have a proper education. When in counsel with the Father before the world was, it was designed that the Lord God should plant a garden for Adam and Eve in Eden, and give them the task of caring for the fruit trees, and cultivating and training the vegetation. Useful labor was to be their safeguard, and it was to be perpetuated through all generations to the close of earth's history. To have a whole-sided education, it is necessary to combine science with practical labor. From infancy children should be trained to do those things that are appropriate for their age and ability. Parents should now encourage their children to become more independent. Serious troubles are soon to be seen upon the earth, and children should be trained in such a way as to be able to meet them. Many parents give a great deal of time and attention to amusing their children, encouraging them to bring all their troubles to them; but children should be trained to amuse themselves, to exercise their minds in devising plans for their own satisfaction, doing the simple things that are natural for them to do" (ST August 13, 1896).

"The children of the wealthy should not be deprived of the great blessing of having something to do to increase the strength of brain and muscle. Work is not a curse, but a blessing. God gave sinless Adam and Eve a beautiful garden to tend. This was pleasant work, and none but pleasant work would have entered our world, had not the first pair transgressed God's commandments. Delicate idleness and selfish gratification make invalids; they can make the life empty and barren in every way. God has not given human beings reason, and crowned their lives with his goodness, that they may be cursed with the sure results of idleness. The wealthy are not to be deprived of the privilege and blessing of a place among the world's workers. They should realize that they are responsible for the use they make of their entrusted possessions; that their strength, their time, and their money, are to be used wisely, and not for selfish purposes" (SpTEd 40, 1897).

"The Sabbath is not to be a gloomy day, a day of unrest and uneasiness. Parents may take their children outdoors, in the groves, in the flower garden, and teach them that the Lord has given them these beautiful things as an expression of his love. Christ has said: 'Consider the lilies of the field, how they grow; they toil not, neither do they spin: and yet I say unto you, That even Solomon in all his glory was not arrayed like one of these. Wherefore, if God so clothe the grass of the field, which to day is, and tomorrow is cast into the oven, shall he not much more clothe you, O ye of little faith? Therefore take no thought, saying, What shall we eat? or, What shall we drink? or, Wherewithal shall we be clothed? (For after all these things do the Gentiles seek:) for your Heavenly Father knoweth that ye have need of all these things. But seek ye first the kingdom of God, and his righteousness; and all these things shall be added unto you. Take therefore no thought for the morrow: for the morrow shall take thought for the things of itself. Sufficient unto the day is the evil thereof'" (RH June 8, 1897).

"Mothers wear out their nerves by doing needless things, in order to keep pace with fashion. One-third of the time now devoted to this work should be spent with their children in the open air, weeding the garden, picking berries, teaching the children to help.

"Enough is wasted on fashionable dress and in the preparation of articles of food that irritate the digestive organs, to purchase a spot of ground, which the children could have as their own, and from which mothers and fathers could derive precious lessons, to be given to their children. Teach your children that the garden in which they place the tiny seed represents the garden of the heart, and that God has enjoined upon you, their parents, to cultivate the soil of their hearts, as they cultivate the garden" (Ms138-1898).

"Teach the children to see Christ in nature. Take them out into the open air, under the noble trees, into the garden; and in all the wonderful works of creation teach them to see an expression of His love. Teach them that He made the laws which govern all living things, that He has made laws for us, and that these laws are for our happiness and joy. Do not weary them with long prayers and tedious exhortations, but through nature's object lessons teach them obedience to the law of God" (DA 516, 1898).

"W. C. White saw Brother Coulston's [a new convert in Australia] necessity, and borrowed eight pounds from our blacksmith and loaned it to him, that he might make a beginning. And all are glad and more than astonished to see the beginning he has made. About twelve acres have been cleared and planted with sweet corn and field corn. The sweet corn they will eat, and the field corn they will sell. The vegetables that have been grown help a great deal in supporting the family. The little lads are working with their father like little farmers. They are so earnest and full of zeal that it is amusing to look at them and see how happy they are in their work. They have not much society besides their own family connections, but they are in the very best school they could be in.

"We feel thankful to God for what we see, and we shall encourage those who come into the truth to take up land which they can cultivate, and so sustain themselves" (Lt48-1899).

"Whenever it is possible, parents should have a piece of land connected with the home, that the children may learn to cultivate the soil. How many beautiful and valuable lessons may be drawn from preparing the ground, sowing the seed, and tending the growing plants. In learning these lessons, parents and children are benefited and blessed" (Ms41-1902).

> *"Whenever it is possible, parents should have a piece of land connected with the home, that the children may learn to cultivate the soil."*

"But it is not God's will that His people shall settle in the cities, where there is constant turmoil and confusion. Their children should be spared this; for the whole system is demoralized by the hurry and rush and noise. The Lord desires His people to move into the country, where they can settle on the land, and raise their own fruit and vegetables, and where their children can be brought in direct contact with the works of God in nature. Take your families away from the cities, is my message" (Lt82-1902).

"So long as God gives me power to speak to our people, I shall continue to call upon parents to leave the cities and get homes in the country, where they can cultivate the soil and learn from the book of nature the lessons of purity and simplicity. The things of nature are the Lord's silent ministers, given to us to teach us spiritual truths. They speak to us of the love of God and declare the wisdom of the great Master-artist" (Lt47-1903).

"If we place ourselves under objectionable influences, can we expect God to work a miracle to undo the results of our wrong course? No, indeed. Get out of the cities as soon as possible, and purchase a little piece of land where you can have a garden, where your children can watch the flowers growing, and learn from them lessons of simplicity and purity. 'Consider the lilies of the field, how they grow; they toil not, neither do they spin: And yet I say unto you, That even Solomon in all his glory was not arrayed like one of these" (Matthew 6:28, 29). Parents, point your children to the beautiful things of God's creation, and from these things teach them of His love for them. Point them to the lovely flowers—the roses and the lilies and the pinks—and then point them to the living God" (Ms10-1903).

"Children should not be long confined within doors, nor should they be required to apply themselves closely to study until a good foundation has been laid for physical development. For the first eight or ten years of a child's life the field or garden is the best schoolroom, the mother the best teacher, nature the best lesson book. Even when the child is old enough to attend school, his health should be regarded as of greater importance than a knowledge of books. He should be surrounded with the conditions most favorable to both physical and mental growth" (Ed 208, 1903).

"Since both men and women have a part in home-making, boys as well as girls should gain a knowledge of household duties. To make a bed and put a room in order, to wash dishes, to prepare a meal, to wash and repair his own clothing, is a training that need not make any boy less manly; it will make him happier and more useful. And if girls, in turn, could learn to harness and drive a horse, and to use the saw and the hammer, as well as the rake and the hoe, they would be better fitted to meet the emergencies of life" (Ed 216, 1903).

"Fathers and mothers, teach your children of the wonder-working power of God. His power is manifest in every plant, in every tree that bears fruit. Take the children into the garden and explain to them how He causes the seed to grow. The farmer plows his land and sows the seed, but he cannot make the seed grow. He must depend upon God to do that which no human power can do. The Lord puts His own Spirit into the seed, causing it to spring into life. Under His care the germ breaks through the case enclosing it and springs up to develop and bear fruit.

"As the children study the great lessonbook of nature, God will impress their minds. As they are told of the work that He does for the seed, they learn the secret of growth in grace. Rightly understood, these lessons lead to the Creator, teaching those simple, holy truths that bring the heart into close touch with God" (8T 326, 1904).

"In building, many make careful provision for their plants and flowers. The greenhouse or window devoted to their use is warm and sunny; for without warmth, air, and sunshine, plants would not live and flourish. If these conditions are necessary to the life of plants, how much more necessary are they for our own health and that of our families and guests!" (MH 275, 1905).

"Where it is possible, the boys and girls should have a piece of land where they can raise something for market, and thus earn means that they can devote to missionary purposes" (Ms65-1908).

"Let parents understand that the training of their children is an important work in the saving of souls. In country places abundant, useful exercise will be found in doing those things that need to be done, and which will give physical health by developing nerve and muscle. 'Out of the cities' is my message for the education of our children" (Ms85-1908).

"In connection with your home, have a garden, if possible, where your children can work and where you can work with them. So instruct them and so arrange their work that their spare time will not be spent in idleness. Give them something definite to do, and let them feel that they are doing something to help father and mother to sustain the family. Let the older ones feel the responsibility of giving a right example to the younger children. Let all act a part according to their years. When the children thus trained attend school, they will have clear minds. They will be able to reason for themselves, and will not accept that which this one says or what that one says without some proof" (Ms33-1909).

"Families and institutions should learn to do more in the cultivation and improvement of land. If people only knew the value of the products of the ground, which the earth brings forth in their season, more diligent efforts would be made to cultivate the soil. All should be acquainted with the special value of fruit and vegetables fresh from the orchard and garden" (Ms13-1911).

"If possible, the home should be out of the city, where the children can have ground to cultivate. Let them each have a piece of ground of their own; and as you teach them how to make a garden, how to prepare the soil for seed, and the importance of keeping all the weeds pulled out, teach them also how important it is to keep unsightly, injurious practices out of the life. Teach them to keep down wrong habits as they keep down the weeds in their gardens. It will take time to teach these lessons, but it will pay, greatly pay.

"Tell your children about the miracle-working power of God. As they study the great lesson book of nature, God will impress their minds. The farmer plows his land and sows his seed, but he cannot make the seed grow. He must depend on God to do that which no human power can do. The Lord puts His vital power into the seed, causing it to spring forth into life. Under His care the germ of life breaks through the hard crust encasing it, and springs up to bear fruit. First appears the blade, then the ear, then the full corn in the ear. As the children are told of the work that God does for the seed, they learn the secret of growth in grace.

"There is untold value in industry. Let the children be taught to do something useful. More than human wisdom is needed that parents may understand how best to educate their children for a useful, happy life here, and for higher service and greater joy hereafter" (CT 124, 125, 1913).

Agriculture and Our Schools

Location of Our Schools
"True missionary workers will not colonize. God's people are to be pilgrims and strangers on the earth. The investment of large sums of money in the building up of the work in one place is not in the order of God. Plants are to be made in many places. Schools and sanitariums are to be established in places where there is now nothing to represent the truth. These interests are not to be established for the purpose of making money, but for the purpose of spreading the truth. Land should be secured at a distance from the cities, on which schools can be built up, and where the youth can be instructed in agricultural and mechanical lines of work" (Ms12-1889).

"The children and youth, all classes of students, need the lessons to be derived from this source. In itself the beauty of nature leads the soul away from sin and worldly attractions and toward purity, peace, and God. For this reason the cultivation of the soil is good work for children and youth. It brings them into direct contact with nature and nature's God. And that they may have this advantage, in connection with our schools there should be, as far as possible, large flower gardens and extensive lands for cultivation.

"An education amid such surroundings is in accordance with the directions which God has given for the instruction of youth; but it is in direct contrast with the methods employed in the majority of schools. Parents and teachers have disregarded the counsel of the Lord. Instead of following the light He has given, they have walked in the sparks of their own kindling. The minds of the young have been occupied with books of science and philosophy, where the thorns of skepticism have been only partially concealed with vague, fanciful fairy stories; or with the works of authors who, although they may write on Scripture subjects, weave in their own fanciful interpretations. The teaching of such books is as seed sown in the heart. It grows and bears fruit, and a plentiful harvest of infidelity is reaped and the result is seen in the depravity of the human family.

> *"Work in the garden and field will be an agreeable change from the wearisome routine of abstract lessons to which their young minds should never be confined."*

"A return to simpler methods will be appreciated by the children and youth. Work in the garden and field will be an agreeable change from the wearisome routine of abstract lessons to which their young minds should never be confined. To the nervous child, who finds lessons from books exhausting and hard to remember, it will be especially valuable. There is health and happiness for him in the study of nature, and the impressions made will not fade out of his mind, for they will be associated with objects that are continually before his eyes.

"God has, in the natural world, placed in the hands of the children of men the key to unlock the treasure house of his world. The unseen is illustrated by the seen; divine wisdom, eternal truth, infinite grace, are understood by the things that God has made. Then let the children and youth become acquainted with nature and nature's laws. Let the mind be developed to the utmost capacity, and the physical powers trained for the practical duties of life. But teach them also that God has made this world fair because he delights in our happiness, and that a more beautiful home is [being] prepared for us in that world where there will be no more sin. The Word of God declares, 'Eye hath not seen, nor ear heard, neither have entered into the heart of man, the things which God hath prepared for them that love him'" (Ms74-1896).

"The reasons that have led us in a few places to turn away from cities and locate our schools in the country, hold good with the schools in other places. To expend money in additional buildings when a school is already deeply in debt is not in accordance with God's plan. Had the money which our larger schools have used in expensive buildings been invested in procuring land where students could receive a proper education, so large a number of students would not now be struggling under the weight of increasing debt, and the work of these institutions would be in a more prosperous condition. Had this course been followed, there would have been some grumbling from students, and many objections would have been raised by parents; but the students would have secured an all-round education, which would have prepared them, not only for practical work in various trades, but for a place on the Lord's farm in the earth made new" (6T 177, 1901).

[Alternate version] "Let the students be out in the most healthful location that can be secured, to do the very work that should have been done years ago. Then there would not be so great discouragements. Had this been done, you would have had some grumbling from students, and many objections would have been raised by parents, but this all-round education would educate the children and youth, not only for practical work in various trades, but would prepare them for the Lord's farm in the earth made new....

"Nature is our lesson book.... There is room in her vast boundaries for schools to be located where grounds can be cleared, land cultivated, and where a proper education can be given. This work is essential for an all-round education, and one which is favorable to spiritual advancement. Nature's voice is the voice of Jesus Christ teaching us innumerable lessons of perseverance. The mountains and hills are changing; the earth is waxing old like a garment, but the blessing of God, which spreads a table for his people in the wilderness, will never cease" (Lt75-1898, to E. A. Sutherland).

"With the question of recreation the surroundings of the home and the school have much to do. In the choice of a home or the location of a school these things should be considered. Those with whom mental and physical well-being is of greater moment than money or the claims and customs of society, should seek for their children the benefit of nature's teaching, and recreation amidst her surroundings. It would be a great aid in educational work could every school be so situated as to afford the pupils land for cultivation, and access to the fields and woods....

"No recreation helpful only to themselves will prove so great a blessing to the children and youth as that which makes them helpful to others. Naturally enthusiastic and impressible, the young are quick to respond to suggestion. In planning for the culture of plants, let the teacher seek to awaken an interest in beautifying the school grounds and the schoolroom.

A double benefit will result. That which the pupils seek to beautify they will be unwilling to have marred or defaced. A refined taste, a love of order, and a habit of care-taking will be encouraged; and the spirit of fellowship and co-operation developed will prove to the pupils a lifelong blessing.

"So also a new interest may be given to the work of the garden or the excursion in field or wood, as the pupils are encouraged to remember those shut in from these pleasant places and to share with them the beautiful things of nature" (Ed 211-213, 1903).

"For breaking the spell of fashion, the teacher can often find no means more effective than contact with nature. Let pupils taste the delights to be found by river or lake or sea; let them climb the hills, gaze on the sunset glory, explore the treasures of wood and field; let them learn the pleasure of cultivating plants and flowers; and the importance of an additional ribbon or ruffle will sink into insignificance" (Ed 247, 1903).

"Be assured that the call is for our people to locate miles away from the large cities. One look at San Francisco as it is today would speak to your intelligent minds, showing you the necessity of getting out of the cities. Do not establish institutions in the cities, but seek a rural location. The call is, 'Come out from among them, and be ye separate.' The very atmosphere of the city is polluted. Let your schools be established away from the cities, where agricultural and other industries can be carried on" (Lt158-1906).

"God wants us to prepare a place for those who shall receive their education, not only in book knowledge, but in agricultural lines, to till the soil; and as they are tilling the soil, they are getting their lessons all the time, how the soil of the Lord should be worked, how they should weed out the wrongs, how they should stir up the fallow ground of the heart, that the seeds of truth may find access to the soil" (Ms139-1906).

"God has revealed to me that we are in positive danger of bringing into our educational mark the customs and fashions that prevail in the schools of the world. If teachers are not guarded in their work, they will place on the necks of their students worldly yokes instead of the yoke of Christ. The plan of the schools we shall establish in these closing years of the work is to be of an entirely different order from those we have instituted in the past.

"For this reason, God bids us establish schools away from the cities, where, without let or hindrance, we can carry on the work of education upon plans that are in harmony with the solemn message that is committed to us for the world. Such an education as this can best be worked out where there is land to cultivate, and where the physical exercise taken by the students can be of such a nature as to act a valuable part in their character building and to fit them for usefulness in the fields to which they will go" (Ms59-1907).

"Light has been given me that in connection with our schools there should be land. This is in harmony with the instruction given regarding the Avondale School, in Australia. Through the industry of man, the land is to be educated, as well as the children. Many of the southern people have lessons to learn in regard to the proper treatment of the land. As our teachers and students care for the land intelligently, they have opportunities to teach lessons on land culture, and the grace of Christ will be with them in all their efforts.

"As matters have been presented before me, I know that most valuable lessons can be learned through contact with the real things of life in connection with a study of books. The acquirement of properties, such as the one mentioned in your letter [in Virginia], gives our people an opportunity to train the physical nature of children, as well as to develop the mental and the moral natures. The possession of land in connection with our schools brings most precious advantages to teachers and students—advantages that all our schools should have, in order to be prepared to give proper instruction" (Lt10-1909).

> *"The possession of land in connection with our schools brings most precious advantages to teachers and students—advantages that all our schools should have."*

Economic Considerations—Does It Pay?

"The objection most often urged against industrial training in the schools is the large outlay involved. But the object to be gained is worthy of its cost. No other work committed to us is so important as the training of the youth, and every outlay demanded for its right accomplishment is means well spent.

"Even from the viewpoint of financial results, the outlay required for manual training would prove the truest economy. Multitudes of our boys would thus be kept from the street corner and the groggery; the expenditure for gardens, workshops, and baths would be more than met by the saving on hospitals and reformatories. And the youth themselves, trained to habits of industry, and skilled in lines of useful and productive labor—who can estimate their value to society and to the nation?" (Ed 18, 1903).

"I urge that our other schools be given encouragement in their efforts to develop plans for the training of the youth in agricultural and other lines of industrial work. When, in ordinary business, pioneer work is done, and preparation is made for future development, there is frequently a financial loss. And as our schools introduce manual training, they, too, may at first incur loss. But let us remember the blessing that physical exercise brings to the students. Many students have died while endeavoring to acquire an education, because they confined themselves too closely to mental effort.

"We must not be narrow in our plans. In industrial training there are unseen advantages, which can not be measured or estimated. Let no one begrudge the effort necessary to carry forward successfully the plan that for years has been urged upon us as of primary importance" (PH164 37, 1904).

"In many minds the question will arise, Can industrial work in our schools be made to pay? and if it cannot, should it be carried forward?

"It would be surprising if industries could be made to pay immediately on being started. Sometimes God permits losses to come to teach us lessons that will keep us from making mistakes that would involve much larger losses. Let those who have had financial losses in their industrial work search carefully to find out the cause and endeavor to manage in such a way that in the future there will be no loss" (CT 315, 1913).

"In their efforts to economize, our brethren should be careful lest they restrict the investment of means where wise investment is needed. In establishing schools and sanitariums, enough land should be purchased to provide for the carrying out of the plans that the Lord has outlined for these institutions. Provision should be made for the raising of fruit and vegetables, and, wherever possible, sufficient land should be secured so that others may not erect, near the institution, buildings of an objectionable character" (GW 457, 1915).

A Balanced Education
"There should have been in past generations provisions made for education upon a larger scale. In connection with the schools should have been agricultural and manufacturing establishments. There should have been teachers also of household labor. There should have been a portion of the time each day devoted to labor, that the physical and mental might be equally exercised. If schools had been established upon the plan we have mentioned, there would not now be so many unbalanced minds" (HR April 1, 1873).

"I have been led to inquire, Must all that is valuable in our youth be sacrificed, in order that they may obtain an education at the schools? The constant strain upon the brain, while the muscles are inactive, enfeebles the nerves, and students have an almost uncontrollable desire for change and exciting amusements. After confinement to study several hours each day, they are, when released, nearly wild....

"If there had been agricultural and manufacturing establishments in connection with our schools, and competent teachers had been employed to educate the youth in the different branches of study and labor, devoting a portion of each day to mental improvement, and a portion of the day to physical labor, there would now be a more elevated class of youth to come upon the stage of action, to have influence in molding society. The youth who would graduate at such institutions would many of them come forth with stability of character. They would have perseverance, fortitude, and courage to surmount obstacles, and principles that would enable them not to be swerved by wrong influence, however popular" (HR September 1, 1873).

"It would be well could there be connected with our College, land for cultivation, and also work-shops, under the charge of men competent to instruct the students in the various departments of physical labor. Much is lost by a neglect to unite physical with mental taxation. The leisure hours of the student are often occupied with frivolous pleasures, which weaken physical, mental, and moral powers. Under the debasing power of sensual indulgence, or the untimely excitement of courtship and marriage, many students fail to reach that height of mental development which they might otherwise have attained" (PH117, 1882).

"Every institution of learning should make provision for the study and practice of agriculture and the mechanic arts. Competent teachers should be employed to instruct the youth in the various industrial pursuits, as well as in the several branches of study. While a part of each day is devoted to mental improvement, let a stated portion be given to physical labor, and a suitable time to devotional exercises and the study of the Scriptures.

"This training would encourage habits of self-reliance, firmness, and decision. Graduates of such institutions would be prepared to engage successfully in the practical duties of life. They would have courage and perseverance to surmount obstacles, and firmness of principle that would not yield to evil influences.

> *"If the youth can have but a one-sided education, which is of the greatest importance, the study of the sciences... or a thorough training in practical duties.... We unhesitatingly say, the latter."*

"If the youth can have but a one-sided education, which is of the greatest importance, the study of the sciences, with all the disadvantages to health and morals, or a thorough training in practical duties, with sound morals and good physical development? We unhesitatingly say, the latter. But with proper effort both may, in most cases, be secured" (FE 72,73, 1923).

"Young persons are naturally active, and if they find no legitimate scope for their pent-up energies after the confinement of the schoolroom, they become restless and impatient of control; they are thus led to engage in the rude, unmanly sports that disgrace so many schools and colleges, and even to plunge into scenes of dissipation. And many who leave their homes innocent, are corrupted by their associations at school. Much could be done to obviate these evils, if every institution of learning would make provision for manual labor on the part of the students,—for actual practice in agriculture and the mechanic arts. Competent teachers should be provided to instruct the youth in various industrial pursuits, as well as in their studies in the school room. While a part of each day is devoted to mental improvement and physical labor, devotional exercises and the study of the Scriptures should not be overlooked.

"Students trained in this manner would have habits of self-reliance, firmness, and perseverance, and would be prepared to engage successfully in the practical duties of life. They would have courage and determination to surmount obstacles, and moral stamina to resist evil influences.

"If young persons can have but one set of faculties disciplined, which is most important, the study of the sciences, with the disadvantages to health and morals under which such knowledge is usually obtained, or a thorough training in practical duties, with sound morals and good physical development? In most cases both may be secured if parents will take a little pains; but if both cannot be had, we would unhesitatingly decide in favor of the latter" (ST August 26, 1886).

"The natural and the spiritual are to be combined in the studies of our schools. The operations of agriculture illustrate the Bible lessons. The laws obeyed by the earth reveal the fact that it is under the masterly power of an infinite God. The same principles run through the spiritual and the natural world. Divorce God and His wisdom from the acquisition of knowledge, and you have a lame, one-sided education, dead to all the saving qualities which give power to man, so that through faith in Christ he is capable of acquiring immortality.

"The author of nature is the author of the Bible. Creation and Christianity have one God" (Lt67-1894).

"Taking a certain course of study is not education. The physical as well as the mental powers must be exercised. Many lessons may be learned in connection with agriculture. Working the soil is one of the best kinds of employment, calling the muscles into action and diverting the mind. The sedentary habits of the student need to be varied by active exercise in some useful labor which will help him to gain an all-sided knowledge of practical life" (Ms53-1896).

"There should be work for all students, whether they are able to pay their way or not; the physical and mental powers should receive proportionate attention. Students should learn to cultivate the land; for this will bring them into close contact with nature" (SpTEd 46, 1896).

"The neglect of some parts of the living machinery, while other parts are put to the tax, and wearied and overworked, makes many youth too weak to resist evil practices. They have little power of self-control. The blood is called too liberally to the brain, and the nervous system is overworked. Exercise should be taken, not in play and amusement merely to please self, but exercise in the science of doing good. There is a science in the use of the hand. In the cultivation of the soil, in building houses, in studying and planning various methods of labor, the brain must be exercised; and students can apply themselves to study to much better purpose when a portion of their time is devoted to physical taxation, wearying the muscles. Nature will then give repose and sweet rest" (Lt103-1897, to E. A. Sutherland).

[Alternate version] "Exercise should be taken, not in play and amusement merely to please self, but exercise that will teach the science of doing good. There is a science in the use of the hand. Students who think that education consists only in book study never make a right use of their hands. They should be taught to do the work that thousands of hands are never educated to do. The powers thus developed and cultivated can be most usefully employed. In the cultivation of the soil, in building houses, in studying and planning various methods of labor, the brain must be exercised, and students can apply themselves to much better purpose when a portion of their time is devoted to physical taxation, wearying the muscles. Nature will then give sweet repose" (YI April 7, 1898).

"If all in America had encouraged the work in agricultural lines that principals and teachers have discouraged, the schools would have had altogether a different showing. Opposing influences would have been overcome; circumstances would have changed; there would have been greater physical and mental strength; labor would have been equalized; and the taxing of all the human machinery would have proved the sum. But the directions God has been pleased to give you, you have taken hold of so gingerly that you have not had the ability to overcome obstacles. It reveals cowardice to move as slowly and uncertainly as you have done in the labor line, for this is the very best kind of education that can be obtained" (Lt75-1898, to E. A. Sutherland).

"Had all our schools encouraged work in agricultural lines, they would now have an altogether different showing. There would not be so great discouragements. Opposing influences would have been overcome; financial conditions would have changed. With the students, labor would have been equalized; and as all the human machinery was proportionately taxed, greater physical and mental strength would have been developed. But the instruction which the Lord has been pleased to give has been taken hold of so feebly that obstacles have not been overcome.

"It reveals cowardice to move so slowly and uncertainly in the labor line—that line which will give the very best kind of education. Look at nature. There is room within her vast boundaries for schools to be established where grounds can be cleared and land cultivated. This work is essential to the education most favorable to spiritual advancement; for nature's voice is the voice of Christ, teaching us innumerable lessons of love and power and submission and perseverance. Some do not appreciate the value of agricultural work. These should not plan for our schools, for they will hold everything from advancing in right lines. In the past their influence has been a hindrance....

"Working the soil is one of the best kinds of employment, calling the muscles into action and resting the mind. Study in agricultural lines should be the A, B, and C of the education given in our schools. This is the very first work that should be entered upon. Our schools should not depend upon imported produce, for grain and vegetables, and the fruits so essential to health. Our youth need an education in felling trees and tilling the soil as well as in literary lines. Different teachers should be appointed to oversee a number of students in their work and should work with them. Thus the teachers themselves will learn to carry responsibilities as burden bearers. Proper students also should in this way be educated to bear responsibilities and to be laborers together with the teachers. All should counsel together as to the very best methods of carrying on the work" (6T 177–179, 1901).

> *"Study in agricultural lines should be the A, B, and C of the education given in our schools."*

"The Lord calls for steps in advance. Because the teachers may never have been trained in physical or manual labor, they are not easily persuaded in regard to the very best methods to secure for the youth an all-round education; and even the very ones who have been the most reluctant to come into line in this matter, had they been given in their youth the physical, mental, and moral education combined, might have saved themselves many attacks of illness, and their brain, bone, and muscle would at this time be in a more healthful condition because all the Lord's machinery would be proportionately taxed. The best instructors should be secured in spiritual lines, in agricultural employments, and also in the carpenter's trade, and in the printing business. The Lord would have these mechanical industries brought in and taught by competent men" (RH January 28, 1902).

"We are to educate the youth to exercise equally the mental and the physical powers. The healthful exercise of the whole being will give an education that is broad and comprehensive. We had stern work to do in Australia in educating parents and youth along these lines; but we persevered in our efforts until the lesson was learned that in order to have an education that was complete, the time of study must be divided between the gaining of book knowledge and the securing of a knowledge of practical work. Part of each day was spent in useful work, the students learning how to clear the land, how to cultivate the soil, and how to build houses, using time that would otherwise have been spent in playing games and seeking amusement. And the Lord blessed the students who thus devoted their time to acquiring habits of usefulness" (RH November 11, 1909).

A Practical Education

"In every school Satan will try to make himself the guide of the teachers who are instructing the students. It is he who would introduce the idea that selfish amusements are a necessity. It is he who would lead students sent to our schools for the purpose of receiving an education and training for the work of evangelists, ministers, and missionaries to believe that amusements are essential to keep them in physical health, when the Lord has presented to them that the better way is for them to embrace manual labor in their education, and thus let useful employment take the place of selfish amusements. These amusements, if followed, soon develop a dislike for useful, healthful exercise of body and mind, such as would make students efficient to serve themselves and others.

"The education to be gained in the felling of trees, the tilling of the soil, and the erection of buildings, as well as the studies of the classroom, is what our youth should seek to obtain. Tent making also should be taught; buildings should be erected; and masonry should be learned. Farther on, a printing press should be connected with the school, that an education may be given to students in this line of work.

"There are many things which the lady students may also engage in, such as cooking, dressmaking, and gardening. Plants and flowers should be cultivated, strawberries should be planted. Thus the lady students may be called out of doors to gain healthful exercise and to be educated in useful labor. Bookbinding also, and a variety of trades should be taken up. These will not only give exercise to brain, bone, and muscle, but they will also give knowledge of great value. The greatest curse of our world today is idleness. The students coming to our school have had an abundance of amusement, which serve merely to please and gratify self. They are now to be given a different education, that they may go forth from the school prepared for any service" (Lt60a-1896).

[Alternate version to middle paragraph] "Students sent to school to prepare to become evangelists, ministers, and missionaries to foreign countries, have received the idea that amusements are essential to keep them in physical health, when the Lord has presented it before them that the better way is to embrace in their education manual labor in place of amusement.... The education to be obtained in felling trees, tilling the soil, as well as in literature, is the education our youth should seek to obtain. Farther on printing-presses should be connected with our schools. Tent making also should be taken hold of. Buildings should be erected, and masonry should be learned" (HL 138, 1897).

"Many who have been educated in our schools are heedless. They do a little here, and a little somewhere else, but they show that they have not been educated for practical work. Students should remember that it is their first interest to make themselves practical, all-round, useful men and women, who in an emergency can do the work necessary to be done. When students are given this kind of education, it will not be necessary to expend money to transport men thousands of miles to plan schools, meeting houses, and colleges.

"Students should be encouraged to combine mental and physical labor. The physical powers should be developed in proportion to the mental faculties. This is essential for an all-round education. They will then be at home in any place. They should be prepared to teach others how to build, how to cultivate the soil, and how to care for orchards. A man may have a brilliant mind, he may be quick to catch ideas, but this is of little value to himself and to others if he has no knowledge of practical work, and if he does not know how to put his ideas into execution. Such a one is only half educated" (Ms61-1897).

> *"Students should be encouraged to combine mental and physical labor.... This is essential for an all-round education."*

"Because difficulties arise, we are not to drop the industries that have been taken hold of as branches of education. While attending school the youth should have an opportunity for learning the use of tools. Under the guidance of experienced workmen, carpenters who are apt to teach, patient, and kind, the students themselves should erect buildings on the school grounds and make needed improvements, thus by practical lessons learning how to build economically. The students should also be trained to manage all the different kinds of work connected with printing, such as typesetting, presswork, and book binding, together with tentmaking and other useful lines of work. Small fruits should be planted, and vegetables and flowers cultivated, and this work the lady students may be called out of doors to do. Thus, while exercising brain, bone, and muscle, they will also be gaining a knowledge of practical life" (6T 176, 1901).

"The students are in our schools for a special training to become acquainted with all lines of work that should they go out as missionaries they could be self-reliant and able, through their educated ability, to furnish themselves with necessary conveniences and facilities. Whether men or women, they should learn to mend, wash, and keep their own clothes in order. They should be able to cook their own meals. They should be familiar with agriculture and with mechanical pursuits. Thus they can lighten their own expenses, and, by their example, inculcate principles of thrift and economy. These lessons can best be taught where economy in all things is conscientiously practiced" (6T 208, 1901).

"Manual training is deserving of far more attention than it has received. Schools should be established that, in addition to the highest mental and moral culture, shall provide the best possible facilities for physical development and industrial training. Instruction should be given in agriculture, manufactures,—covering as many as possible of the most useful trades,— also in household economy, healthful cookery, sewing, hygienic dressmaking, the treatment of the sick, and kindred lines. Gardens, workshops, and treatment rooms should be provided, and the work in every line should be under the direction of skilled instructors.

"The work should have a definite aim and should be thorough. While every person needs some knowledge of different handicrafts, it is indispensable that he become proficient in at least one. Every youth, on leaving school, should have acquired a knowledge of some trade or occupation by which, if need be, he may earn a livelihood....

"As a relaxation from study, occupations pursued in the open air, and affording exercise for the whole body, are the most beneficial. No line of manual training is of more value than agriculture. A greater effort should be made to create and to encourage an interest in agricultural pursuits. Let the teacher call attention to what the Bible says about agriculture: that it was God's plan for man to till the earth; that the first man, the ruler of the whole world, was given a garden to cultivate; and that many of the world's greatest men, its real nobility, have been tillers of the soil. Show the opportunities in such a life. The wise man says, 'The king himself is served by the field.' Ecclesiastes 5:9. Of him who cultivates the soil the Bible declares, 'His God doth instruct him to discretion, and doth teach him.' Isaiah 28:26.

And again, 'Whoso keepeth the fig tree shall eat the fruit thereof.' Proverbs 27:18. He who earns his livelihood by agriculture escapes many temptations and enjoys unnumbered privileges and blessings denied to those whose work lies in the great cities. And in these days of mammoth trusts and business competition, there are few who enjoy so real an independence and so great certainty of fair return for their labor as does the tiller of the soil.

"In the study of agriculture, let pupils be given not only theory, but practice. While they learn what science can teach in regard to the nature and preparation of the soil, the value of different crops, and the best methods of production, let them put their knowledge to use. Let teachers share the work with the students, and show what results can be achieved through skillful, intelligent effort. Thus may be awakened a genuine interest, an ambition to do the work in the best possible manner. Such an ambition, together with the invigorating effect of exercise, sunshine, and pure air, will create a love for agricultural labor that with many youth will determine their choice of an occupation. Thus might be set on foot influences that would go far in turning the tide of migration which now sets so strongly toward the great cities" (Ed 218–220, 1903).

"Those who go forth from our schools to engage in mission work will have need of an experience in the cultivation of the soil and in various lines of manual labor. They should receive a training that will fit them to take hold of any line of work in the fields to which they shall be called. No work will be more effectual than that done by those who, having obtained an education in practical life, go forth prepared to instruct as they have been instructed. In His teachings the Saviour represented the world as a vineyard. We would do well to study the parables in which this figure is used. If in our schools the land were more faithfully cultivated, the buildings more disinterestedly cared for by the students, the love of sports and amusements, which cause so much perplexity in our school work, would pass away" (Ms99-1907).

"Students should be given a practical education in agriculture. This will be of inestimable value to many in their future work. The training to be obtained in felling trees and in tilling the soil, as well as in literary lines, is the education that our youth should seek to obtain. Agriculture will open resources for self-support. Other lines of work, adapted to different students, may also be carried on. But

> *"We should so train the youth that they will love to engage in the cultivation of the soil."*

the cultivation of the land will bring a special blessing to the workers. We should so train the youth that they will love to engage in the cultivation of the soil" (CT 311, 1913).

Counsel to Teachers
"Let the teachers in our schools take their students with them into the gardens and fields, and teach them how to work the soil in the very best manner.... Both teachers and students would have much more healthful experience in spiritual things, and much stronger minds and purer hearts to interpret eternal mysteries, than they can have while studying books so constantly, and working the brain without taxing the muscles. God has given men and women reasoning powers, and He would have men employ their reason in regard to the use of their physical machinery. The question may be asked, How can he get wisdom that holdeth the plow, and driveth oxen? By seeking her as silver, and searching for her as for hid treasures. 'For his God doth instruct him to discretion, and doth teach him.' 'This also cometh forth from the Lord of Hosts, which is wonderful in counsel, and excellent in working'" (Ms8a-1894).

"By a study of natural things they [Christian teachers] may exemplify spiritual things. The Lord has given the open book of nature in material substances. In the tilling of the soil, proper persons should be appointed to oversee a certain number of students, and should work with them. Thus the teachers themselves will be helped to become men who can carry responsibilities as burden-bearers. The Lord Himself gives His presence to this line of education....

"Students should not merely be told to do this or do that, without being given a lesson that will teach them the principles underlying the things they are required to do.... As they put seeds into the ground, teach them the lesson of the germinating principle of seeds, found in the great Lesson Book. Teach them the time to sow, the time to plant trees in their season and when to prune them. Draw lessons from the day and night, the sunshine and clouds, the former and the latter rains, the harvest" (Ms55-1898).

"Let the teachers in our school wake up, and impart the knowledge they have in agricultural lines, and in the industries that it is essential for the students to understand,—seek in every line of labor to reach the very best results. Let the science of the word of God be brought into the work, that the students may understand correct principles, and may reach the highest possible standard. Exert your God-given abilities, and bring all your energies into the development of the Lord's farm. Study and labor, that the best results and the greatest returns may come from the seed sowing, that there may be an abundant supply of food, both temporal and spiritual" (Advocate February 1, 1899).

Physical Benefits to the Students
"Where useful labor is combined with study, there is no need of gymnastic exercises; and much more benefit is derived from work performed in the open air than from indoor exercise. The farmer and the mechanic each have physical exercise; yet the farmer is much the healthier of the two, for nothing short of the invigorating air and sunshine will fully meet the wants of the system. The farmer finds in his labor all the movements that were ever practiced in the gymnasium. And his movement room is the open fields; the canopy of heaven is its roof, and the solid earth its floor. A farmer who is temperate in all his habits usually enjoys good health. His work is pleasant; and his vigorous exercise causes full, deep, and strong inspirations and exhalations, which expand the lungs and purify the blood, sending the warm current of life bounding through arteries and veins.

"In what contrast to the habits of the active farmer are those of the student who neglects physical exercise. The student sits day after day in a close room, bending over his desk or table, his chest contracted, his lungs crowded. His brain is taxed to the utmost, while his body is inactive. He cannot take full, deep inspirations; his blood moves sluggishly; his feet are cold, his head hot. How can such a person have health? It is not hard study that is destroying the health of students, so much as it is their disregard of nature's laws. Let them take regular exercise that will cause them to breathe deep and full, and they will soon feel that they have a new hold on life" (ST August 26, 1886).

"Nature will not be imposed upon. She will not forgive the injuries done to the wonderful, delicate machinery. The pale, weak student is a continual reproach to health reform. Far better would it be for some to go outdoors, and work in the soil. Exercise is good. God designed that all parts of the human machinery should be worked. There should be regular hours for working, regular hours for eating. Without studying the exact cost of every article of food and providing the cheapest kind, procure those articles of food that are the best for making steam to run the living machinery. There is no extravagance in providing the articles of food that the system can best take and digest, and send vitality to every part of the living organism, that all may be nourished" (MMis May 1, 1899).

"Where students are blessed with an opportunity to combine mental and moral training with the training of their physical being, the Lord's plan, as instituted in Eden, may be carried out. In Genesis we read: 'The Lord God planted a garden eastward in Eden; and there He put the man whom He had formed. And out of the ground made the Lord God to grow every tree that is pleasant to the sight, and good for food; the tree of life also in the midst of the garden, and the tree of knowledge of good and evil.... And the Lord God took the man, and put him into the garden of Eden to dress it and to keep it.'

"From this passage of Scripture we learn that suitable employment was given the first human beings that God formed on this earth. He gave them an opportunity to employ their physical powers in the work of dressing the garden, and of keeping it.

"After their fall through disobedience, the Lord sent Adam and Eve out from the garden of Eden; and Adam was instructed to till the ground from whence he had been taken. God wisely provided that a portion of their time and strength should be used in manual work. This is one of His appointed means of aiding them in recovering that which they had lost by their fall.

"'And Abel was a keeper of sheep, but Cain was a tiller of the ground.' Read carefully the fourth chapter of Genesis. In this Scripture the whole story is told. And in the chapters that follow we are told of the work of God in destroying the world because of a departure from His plain commands, which resulted in the world's being filled with transgression and sin.

"Thus we see that God provided for the healthful employment of the physical powers of man even in Eden; and that immediately after the fall, our first parents were given an industry—the tilling of the soil. After the earth was cursed, it brought forth thistles, and thus increased the work of those who till the soil. But the ground was to be tilled by our first parents, and thus one of the purposes of God in creating the earth was fulfilled—the wise employment of the physical powers of its occupants.

"The Lord would have the members of the human family today perform useful labor in the exercise of brain, bone, and muscle. The mind, the hands, the whole physical being must act their appointed part in the lifework. And so, in planning for the establishment of new schools along right lines, we must so arrange matters that the brain power of the students will be developed and strengthened by means of manual training. Thus the muscles and nerves of the body will be trained to obey the action of a healthful brain, and men and women will become workers together with God, the Maker of the world....

"Those who have been trained in a practical way will be able to teach others how to build houses, and how to educate properly the land so that it will produce its treasures" (Lt10-1909).

Counsel for Specific Schools
Battle Creek College, MI - Est. 1874

"I rejoiced when I heard that the Battle Creek school was to be established in a farming district. I know that there will be less temptation there for the students than there would be in the cities that are fast becoming as Sodom and Gomorrah, preparing for destruction by fire. The popular sentiment is that cities should be chosen as locations for our schools. But God desires us to leave the sin-polluted atmosphere of the cities. It is His design that our schools shall be established where the atmosphere is purer" (Ms67-1901).

"The light that has been given me is that Battle Creek has not the best influence over the students in our school. There is altogether too congested a state of things. The school, although it will mean a fewer number of students, should be moved out of Battle Creek. Get an extensive tract of land, and there begin the work which I entreated should be commenced before our school was established here,—to get out of the cities, to a place where the students would not see things to remark upon and criticise, where they would not see the wayward course of this one and that one, but would settle down to diligent study" (GCB April 14, 1901).

"Greater results would have appeared if a portion of the time and energy bestowed on the large school in Battle Creek to keep it in a healthy condition had been used for schools in other localities where there is room for agricultural pursuits to be carried on as a part of the education. Had there been a willingness to follow the Lord's ways and His plans, many plants would now be growing in other places" (6T 211, 1901).

Pacific Union College - Est. in Healdsburg CA in 1882
(moved to Angwin in 1909)

"If in the past those in charge of the Healdsburg school had had spiritual foresight, they would have secured the land near the school home which is now occupied by houses. The failure to furnish the students with outdoor employment, in the cultivation of the soil, is making their advancement in spirituality very slow and imperfect. The result of this neglect should lead the teachers to be wise unto salvation. It is a mistake for so many dwelling-houses to be crowded close to the school home. This is working greatly to the disadvantage of the students. A lack of wisdom was shown by the failure to secure the land round the school home. This will make the work of preserving order and maintaining discipline harder than it otherwise would be. But order must be preserved at any cost, and the workers in the school must plan how this shall be done most successfully" (Ms11-1901).

> *"The failure to furnish the students with outdoor employment, in the cultivation of the soil, is making their advancement in spirituality very slow and imperfect.*

"Our school should be located where the students can receive an education broader than that which the mere study of books will give. They must have such a training as will fit them for acceptable service if they are called to do pioneer work in mission fields either in America or in foreign countries. There must be land enough to give an experience in the cultivation of the soil and to help largely in making the institution self-supporting" (Ms9-1909).

"I am very glad that we need be delayed no longer in locating our school, and I am more thankful than I can express, that our school and our sanitarium can be near enough together that their educational work may blend. The school can help the sanitarium by supplying it with fruit and vegetables, and the sanitarium can help the school by purchasing these things. And the students may receive advantages from both these institutions.

"I was able to see only the buildings and their immediate surroundings. Those who have seen the orchards and the large tract of timber can speak of these things. I know that the land near the buildings is good and produces abundantly. The fruit raised in the orchard is excellent. And fruit is of great value. In our schools we should study simplicity in diet. There need not be a large amount of troublesome labor put forth in order to make food palatable. When we are really hungry, we shall be able to relish the simple foods that God has furnished. It will be a great advantage to raise on our own school land a large part at least of the fruits, grains, and vegetables that will be necessary for those in the institution" (Ms59-1909).

Oakwood Industrial School, AL - Est. 1896
(now Oakwood University)

"Early on Monday morning we took the train for Huntsville. We reached the school at one o'clock the same day. That afternoon we were taken over a portion of the school farm. We find that there are nearly four hundred acres of land, a large part of which is under cultivation. Several years ago Brother S. M. Jacobs was in charge of the farm, and under his care it made great improvement. He set out a peach and plum orchard and other fruit trees. Brother and Sister Jacobs left Huntsville about three years ago, and since then the farm has not been so well cared for. We see in the land promise of a much larger return than it now gives, were its managers given the help they need....

"Recently the suggestion has been made that the school at Huntsville is too large, and perhaps it would be better to sell the property there and establish the school elsewhere. But in the night season instruction was given me that this farm must not be sold. The Lord's money was invested in the Huntsville school farm to provide a place for the education of colored students. The General Conference gave this land to the Southern work, and the Lord has shown me what this school may become and what those may become who go there for instruction if His plans are followed....

"Wise plans are to be laid for the cultivation of the land. The students are to be given a practical education in agriculture. This education will be of inestimable value to them in their future work. Thorough work is to be done in cultivating the land, and from this the students are to learn how necessary it is to do thorough work in cultivating the garden of the heart" (Lt215-1904).

"The Huntsville school farm is a most beautiful place, and with the three hundred acres of land, much should be accomplished in industrial training and in the raising of crops. The teachers in our schools should remember that they are not only to give the students lessons from books. They are to teach them how to earn their own living by honest work" (Lt337-1904).

"I feel so grateful that we have this farm on which to carry on our school work. I am so glad that it is land which will produce. But it cannot be expected to produce fruit if it is left uncultivated. From this we may learn a spiritual lesson. 'It is My Father's good pleasure,' Christ says to His disciples, 'that ye bear much fruit.' But you cannot bear much fruit unless you take out of your lives the weeds of evil, and let the word of truth dwell in you richly, that your lives may produce the fruits of righteousness and holiness. If you will do this, you will see in the kingdom of God the result of what you have learned on this school farm. Pull up the weeds, and plant the seeds of truth" (Ms60-1904).

"The Huntsville school has been presented to me as being in a very desirable location. It would be difficult to secure another location as promising as the school farm now secured. The buildings and everything connected with the work there should be in harmony with the high and sacred work to be done there. Let there be nothing unsightly connected with the buildings or about the farm, nothing that would indicate slackness.

"If the land is well cared for, it will produce abundantly. Let the teacher go out, taking with them small companies of students, and teach these students how properly to work the soil. Let all those connected with the school study to see how they may improve the property. Teach the students to keep the gardens free from weeds.... Let the care and cultivation of the land of the Huntsville school show to unbelievers that Seventh-day Adventists are reliable and that their influence is of value in the community. The sight of a farm, unproductive because of neglect, has a tendency to belittle the influence of the school.

"The farm, if worked intelligently, is capable of furnishing fruit and other produce for the school. The teachers, both in their work in the schoolroom and on the farm should constantly seek to reach a higher standard, that they may be better able to teach the students how to care for the trees, the berries, the vegetables, and the grains that shall be raised. This will be pleasing to God and will bring the approval and respect of those in the community who understand the principles of agriculture....

"Let us remember that the land is God's property to be worked energetically to His glory. The trees and grains and vegetables will yield their fruit in proportion to the labor that is put forth in their care....

"Several acres of land should at the right time be set out to tomatoes. Young plants should be ready to be transplanted as early as possible. Such a crop would be valuable and might be used to good advantage. Let everything reveal religious thrift" (Ms12-1905).

"All that is done by those connected with the Huntsville school, whether they be teachers or students, is to be done with the realization that this is the Lord's institution, in which the students are to be taught how to cultivate the land, and how to labor for the uplifting of their own people. They are to work with such earnestness and perseverance that the farm will bear testimony to the world, to angels, and to men, regarding the fidelity with which this gift of land has been cared for. This is the Lord's farm, and it is to bear fruit to his glory. Heavenly angels will be able to read, in the thrift and painstaking effort revealed in the care of the farm, the story of the improvement made by the students themselves in character-building. On this farm the students are to learn how to earn their living by honest work. Such a knowledge will be of inestimable value to them when they go forth to teach others of their race" (RH September 21, 1905).

"At the Huntsville school a thorough work is to be done in training men to cultivate the soil and to grow fruits and vegetables. Let no one despise this work. Agriculture is the ABC of industrial education" (Lt289-1907).

"The work done in the Huntsville School is to be an object lesson of what can be done for the colored youth and children in every school, small or large, in providing advantages and surroundings that will tend to uplift and ennoble those who attend. The Huntsville School is to be a place where the standard is kept high. The teachers must be filled with a determination to teach the students, in connection with book-knowledge, practical lessons of neatness and refinement. Nothing coarse or slovenly is to be allowed in the dress of the students. Their deportment is to be above reproach. They are to be taught to be neat in their habits. And in all that pertains to the premises of the school, both inside the various buildings, and on the school-grounds and the farm, an object lesson of orderliness and thrift is to be taught" (GH October 1, 1907).

Avondale College, Australia - Est. 1897
"I have been troubled over many things in regard to our school. In their work the young men are associated with the young women, and are doing the work which belongs to women. This is nearly all that can be found for them to do as they are now situated; but from the light given me, this is not the kind of education that the young men need. It does not give them the knowledge they need to take with them to their homes. There should be a different kind of labor opened before them, that would give opportunity

to keep the physical powers taxed equally with the mental. There should be land for cultivation....

"Here is opened a field to give vent to their pent-up energies, that, if not expended in useful employment, will be a continual source of trial to themselves and to their teachers. Many kinds of labor adapted to different persons may be devised. But the working of the land will be a special blessing to the worker. There is [a] great want of intelligent men to till the soil, who will be thorough. This knowledge will not be a hindrance to the education essential for business or for usefulness in any line. To develop the capacity of the soil requires thought and intelligence. Not only will it develop muscle, but capability for study, because the action of brain and muscle is equalized. We should so train the youth that they would love to work upon the land, and delight in improving it. The hope of advancing the cause of God in this country is in creating a new moral taste in love of work, which will transform mind and character. (Ms8a-1894).

"No one needs to have regret in reference to this land, for with proper working it will surprise the people in this section of the country. All the regret I have is that we have not money to take in sections of the land that would extend the ground. I have not one doubt in reference to the securing of this land. If the Lord prospers those who occupy it and who cultivate it, as we believe He will, we shall see a change that will surprise all who look upon it. I can hardly endure the thought that time is passing, and that the work of clearing the land is delayed.

"I have walked over the most of the O'Leary land. It has been cultivated and should be included in the school land. Someone should be at work upon it, cultivating it. If it could be purchased for any reasonable sum, I would not object to securing the place as a home for myself, if it was thought advisable to do so. No time should be lost in cultivating the land. In the dream you have heard me relate, words were spoken of land which I was looking at, and after deep ploughing and thorough cultivating, it brought forth a bountiful harvest. Having had this matter presented to me at different times, I am more than ever convinced that this is the right location for the school. Since I have been here for a few days and have an opportunity to investigate, I feel more sure than at my first visit that this is the right place. I think any land which I have seen will produce some kind of a crop.

"We cannot expect to find Eden, the Garden of God, in this sin-desecrated earth. There will always be something to mar the most desirable place; but we do see in this land, if not faultless, a favorable place for the location of our school. These grounds will furnish the very best of gymnasiums for our young men, and for our teachers as well. Those who educate the youth in book knowledge need physical exercise to strengthen the muscles as much as do our students. Our teachers need to educate far more from nature than they do. Nature is God's great school, and on these grounds resources are found for acquiring greater knowledge of the wonderful works of God. Advantages procured by locating in this place are not presented to the teachers in such abundance in other places. Here is God's great farm" (Ms35-1894).

"In the school that is started here in Cooranbong, we look to see real success in agricultural lines, combined with a study of the sciences. We mean for this place to be a center, from which shall irradiate light, precious advanced knowledge that shall result in the working of unimproved lands, so that hills and valleys shall blossom like the rose. For both children and men, labor combined with mental taxation will give the right kind of all-round education. The cultivation of the mind will bring tact and fresh incentive to the cultivation of the soil" (Lt47a-1895).

"Well, the school has made an excellent beginning. The students are learning how to plant trees, strawberries, etc.; how they must keep every sprangle and fiber of the roots uncramped in order to give them a chance to grow. Is not this a most precious lesson as to how to treat the human mind, and the body as well? not to cramp any of the organs of the body, but give them ample room to do their work? The mind must be called out, its energies taxed. We want men and women who can be energized by the Spirit of God, to do a complete work under the Spirit's guidance. But these minds must be cultivated, employed, not lazy and dwarfed by inaction. Just so men and women and children are wanted who will work the land, and use their tact and skill, not with a feeling that they are menials, but that they are doing just such noble work as God gave to Adam and Eve in Eden, who loved to see the miracles wrought by the divine husbandman. The human agent plants the seed, and God waters it, and causes his sun to shine upon it, and up springs the tiny blade. Here is the lesson God gives to us concerning the resurrection of the body, and the renewing of the heart. We are to learn of spiritual things from the development of the earthly" (SpTA04 17, 1895).

"We are educating the people here, who are not inclined to put brain, bone, and muscle into their work, that it must become a fixed conviction in their own souls, that religion merely handed down to our fathers will not withstand the temptations of Satan.

"We are trying to demonstrate to them that, while there is no panoply but truth for us in order to be saved, diligence in business is essential to guard us against temptation. Indolence and idleness, games and parties and holiday picnics, are opening many avenues to temptation. Doing away with these abundant pleasure gatherings, and making precious time tell in doing something useful in the service of Christ, will be a greater educating force to make all-sided students than loading down the mind with the studies of authors usually studied in our schools.

"It is not toil in trades, or in cultivation of the soil, that degrades any man; it is not hard, taxing labor that weakens the brain power and creates sickness and disease; it is the little use made of the living machinery that enfeebles, and causes disease and premature death. Disuse of the organs that God has given to the living human agent is the cause of disease and feebleness of all the powers, the intellect included.

"Adam was created in innocency; yet God gave him employment, to tend the garden. This did not degrade him. Here was his book of study—God in nature. He was to study God and obey Him. Paul had to work, laboring with his hands, and felt no dishonor in it. All who would resist temptations that assail them from without and within must make sure that they are on the Lord's side; that His truth is in their hearts; that it keeps sentinel watch in their souls, ready to sound an alarm and summon them to action in warring against every evil.

"All knowledge that deserves the name of science is found in the higher education in the Word of God, and should be acquired by all human agents. True education strengthens the moral powers, expands the mind, and should be cultivated. But the grand educating book, found in nature, which hears and sees God, has been greatly neglected. God help us to teach correctly what constitutes an all-sided education (Lt121-1896).

"We have been moving forward here in Cooranbong in the work which the Lord has signified should be done. He has shown that we should in our preparation and building for the school be giving an education to the workers, combining physical labor with the taxation of the brain. This will give a strength and vigor to the brain that it could not otherwise have.

"We considered this the place where the school should be located, and commenced work at once to the plan which God has specified. The

Agriculture and Our Schools

students are to be laborers as well as learners. The land is to be cleared and cultivated, and trees planted in the grounds. I commenced building my house, and when the foundation was laid, I also had preparations made for raising fruit and vegetables. The light given me of the Lord is that the poverty that exists in this region need not be, for with industry the soil can be cultivated. Moments are not to be wasted in idleness. Our time is the Lord's, and is as precious as gold. When it is carefully treasured and put to use, it will show important results. If properly worked, the land will yield its treasures.

"When we first came to this place with the object of securing land to put up buildings, we were able to realize the inconvenience of depending on Sydney or Newcastle for our vegetables and fruit. They came to us from the market, we paying for the fruit and also four shillings a shipment to the man who was employed to buy and ship to us. This we considered a moderate price. Then frequently when the fruit would come to us so that it would have to lie over Sabbath and in the hot weather much of it spoiled. We knew that with a large family of students, we could not well work in this way. There must be trees planted and a good orchard of such fruits as peaches, apricots, oranges, lemons, apples, and other fruits. We did this at once. The trees in the school orchard and mine, were planted about the last of September, 1895. In September 1896 these trees were in blossom, and in November we ate fruit from them.

"This move was considered a wise one, and now we have thrifty orchards. For the good of the trees we stripped them of nearly all their fruit this year, leaving only specimens of each kind. These specimens were most excellent. This move we believe to be right. It cost money to clear the acres of land to put into orchard, but no more than we could expect" (Lt86-1897).

"The school was established at a great expense, both of time and labor, to enable students to obtain an all-round education, that they might gain a knowledge of agriculture, a knowledge of the common branches of education, and above all, a knowledge of the Word of God" (Lt145-1897).

"After looking well, we decided to engage in the experiment of clearing, and planting trees and seeds immediately when the ground was ready.

"We employed the students then obtaining an education. There were Bible studies in the morning. I attended these morning meetings at six o'clock and gave morning talks to the students, and the Lord was indeed present in our assembly as we addressed the students after a season of most earnest prayer. Then all went forth to their labors in clearing the ground selected for the school buildings. They worked until about two o'clock, then took their dinner and enjoyed it. At three their studies commenced. Their testimony was that they could advance in their studies fully as fast as when they did nothing in the line of physical labor. They were fully convinced that agricultural, out-of-door employment combined with studies would be of far more benefit to them than merely studying alone. They were getting an education essential for practical life, and for physical improvement, by exercising all their God-given faculties of mind and nerve and muscle. Some of these students who could be spared commenced their work in clearing and making a road in the woods to connect with the government road, while others were clearing grounds for building and to put into fruit trees and for planting our vegetable seeds" (Lt161-1897).

"The school located in Avondale is to be conducted in accordance with the mind and will of God. Every student should work from principle, his motto being, I study for time and for eternity; I use my muscles to do the very things that some one must do. Students should perform physical labor in the early morning and in the cool of the day, using the hours during the heat of the day for study. The limbs and muscles are God's gifts just as verily as are riches or intellect. Every part of the human machinery must be used proportionately, or else some parts will be clogged and enfeebled" (Ms84-1897).

"Plans were laid to build cottages on the school campus. I was glad I was here at the time that this subject was brought up, for I had something to say. I told them that the grounds were not to be occupied by buildings.

"The land is to be our lesson book. After being cleared, it is to be cultivated. Orange, lemon, peach, apricot, nectarine, plum, and apple trees are to occupy the land, with vegetable gardens, flower gardens, and ornamental trees. Thus this place is to be brought as near as possible to the presentation that passed before me several times, as the symbol of what our school and premises should be. Dwelling houses, fenced allotments for families were not to be near our school buildings. This place must by the appointment of God be a representation of what school premises should be—a delight to the eye.

"The open book of nature is to be the student's study. Schools should be established away from the cities. I have more invested in this land than any other person. I am carrying students through school paying their expenses that they may get a start. This gives me an influence with teachers and learners. The land was laid out in lots. Houses were to be built, as in a village. But I tell them that buildings are not to be crowded upon the land round the school buildings. This is God's farm, and it is sacred ground. Here the students are to learn the lesson, 'Ye are God's husbandry; ye are God's building.' The work that is done in the land is to be done in a particular, thorough, wise manner. From the cultivation of the soil and the planting of seed lessons in spiritual lines may be learned" (Lt84-1898).

'Before I visited Cooranbong, the Lord gave me a dream. In my dream I was taken to the land that was for sale in Cooranbong. Several of our brethren had been solicited to visit the land, and I dreamed that I was walking upon the ground. I came to a neat-cut furrow that had been ploughed one quarter of a yard deep and two yards in length. Two of the brethren who had been acquainted with the rich soil of Iowa were standing before this furrow and saying, 'This is not good land; the soil is not favorable.' But One who has often spoken in counsel was present also, and He said, 'False witness has been borne of this land.' Then He described the properties of the different layers of earth. He explained the science of the soil, and said that this land was adapted to the growth of fruit and vegetables, and that if well worked would produce its treasures for the benefit of man. This dream I related to Brother and Sister Starr and my family.

"The next day we were on the cars, on our way to meet others who were investigating the land; and as I was afterward walking on the ground where the trees had been removed, lo, there was a furrow just as I had described it, and the men also who had criticized the appearance of the land. The words were spoken just as I had dreamed.

"After we had returned to the cottage rented by one of the brethren for the time we should spend in investigating the land, a council was held, and the decision made to take the land....

"But after this there was a change in the minds of the brethren. They objected to the land, and kept searching for a better location; but in every place there was something objectionable, and they could not come to a decision. I was so sure that the Lord was leading us to locate on these grounds that I told my son Willie and my brethren that I would pay the price for the land myself; then, if they did not want it, I would settle upon it some of our poor brethren who were crowded into the cities. I would make homes here for those who could not make homes for themselves. But this proposition was not acceptable, and for a year the work was greatly hindered by the unbelief of those who should have had faith" (Ms62-1898).

"From the light given me in regard to the location and building up of our school interests, I know that it is the purpose of God that this institution be established at a distance from the city that is so full of temptations and snares, of amusements and holidays, which are not conducive to purity and piety and religious devotion. He designs that we shall connect manual labor with the improvement of the mental powers. I have been shown that study in agricultural lines should be the A B and C of the educational work of our schools. This institution must not depend upon imported produce for the fruits so essential to healthfulness, and for their grains and vegetables. This is the very first work that must be entered upon. Then as we shall advance and add to our facilities, advance studies and object lessons should come in. We are not to subtract from that which has already been taken hold of as a branch of education....

"All the arts are to come into the education of the students. Even in the school at Avondale there are too many studies taken by the students. The youth should not be left to take all the studies they shall choose, for they will be inclined to take more than they can carry; and if they do this, they cannot possibly come from the school with a thorough knowledge of each study. There should be less study of books, and greater painstaking effort made to obtain that knowledge which is essential for practical life. The youth are to learn how to work interestedly and intelligently, that, wherever they are, they may be respected because they have a knowledge of those arts which are so essential for practical life. In the place of being day laborers, under an overseer, they are to strive to be masters of their trades, to place themselves where they can command wages as good carpenters, printers, or as educators in agricultural work" (Ms105-1898).

> *"There should be less study of books, and greater painstaking effort made to obtain that knowledge which is essential for practical life."*

"The educational advantages of our school are to be of a distinct order. This school farm is God's lessonbook. Those who till the soil and plant and cultivate the orchard are to make the application of nature's lessons, and bring these lessons learned into their actual spiritual experience. Let every individual bear in mind that 'whatsoever a man soweth, that shall he also reap.' The man who day by day sows objectionable seeds, in words, in deportment, in spirit, is conforming himself to the same character, and this is determining the future harvest he will reap" (Ms116-1898).

"Let the lands near the school and the church be retained. Those who come to settle in Cooranbong can, if they choose, find for themselves homes near by, or on portions of, the Avondale estate. But the light given me is that all that section of land from the school orchard to the Maitland road, and extending on both sides of the road from the meetinghouse to the school, should become a farm and a park, beautiful with fragrant flowers and ornamental trees. There should be orchards, and every kind of produce should be cultivated that is adapted to the soil, that this place may become an object lesson to those living close by and afar off.

"Then let everything not essential to the work of the school be kept at a distance, and thus prevent any disturbance of the sacredness of the place through the proximity of families and buildings. Let the school stand alone. There must not be this one and that one claiming personal property near it. It will be better for private families, however devoted they may be in the service of the Lord, to be located at some distance from the school buildings. The school is the Lord's property, and the grounds about it are His farm, where the great Sower can make His garden a lessonbook. The results of the labors will be seen, 'first the blade, then the ear, after that the full corn in the ear.' The land will yield its treasures, bringing the joyousness of an abundant harvest, and the produce gathered through the blessing of God is to be used as nature's lessonbook, from which spiritual lessons can be made plain and applied to the necessities of the soul" (Ms170-1899).

"On several occasions the light has come to me that the land around our school is to be used as the Lord's farm. In a special sense portions of this farm should be highly cultivated. Spread out before me I saw land planted with every kind of fruit tree that will bear fruit in this locality; there were also vegetable gardens, where seeds were sown and cultivated.

"If the managers of this farm and the teachers in the school will receive the Holy Spirit to work with them, they will have wisdom in their management, and God will bless their labors. The care of the trees, the planting and the sowing, and the gathering of the harvest are to be wonderful lessons for all the students. The invisible links which connect the sowing and the reaping are to be studied, and the goodness of God is to be pointed out and appreciated. It is the Lord that gives the virtue and the power to the soil and to the seed. Were it not for the divine agency, combined with human tact and ability, the seed sown would be useless. There is an unseen power constantly at work in man's behalf to feed and to clothe him. The parable of the seed as studied in the daily experience of teacher and student is to reveal that God is at work in nature, and it is to make plain the things of the kingdom of heaven" (6T 185, 1901).

"Let the teachers wake up to the importance of this subject and teach agriculture and other industries that it is essential for the students to understand. Seek in every department of labor to reach the very best results. Let the science of the word of God be brought into the work, that the students may understand correct principles and may reach the highest possible standard. Exert your God-given abilities, and bring all your energies into the development of the Lord's farm. Study and labor, that the best results and the greatest returns may come from the seed sowing, that there may be an abundant supply of food, both temporal and spiritual, for the increased number of students that shall be gathered in to be trained as Christian workers.

"We have seen the giant trees felled and uprooted; we have seen the plowshare pressed into the earth, turning deep furrows for the planting of trees and the sowing of seed. The students are learning what plowing means and that the hoe and the shovel, the rake and the harrow, are all implements of honorable and profitable industry. Mistakes will often be made, but every error lies close beside the truth. Wisdom will be learned by failures, and the energy that will make a beginning gives hope of success in the end. Hesitation will keep things back, precipitancy will alike retard; but all will serve as lessons if the human agent will have it so" (6T 191, 192, 1901).

"The cultivation of our land requires the exercise of all the brain power and tact we possess. The unworked lands around us testify to the indolence of men. We hope to arouse to action the dormant senses. We hope to see intelligent farmers who will be rewarded for their earnest labor. The hand and head must co-operate, bringing new and sensible plans into operation in the cultivation of the soil" (Advocate March 1, 1901).

"Every term of school which we have held at Avondale has resulted in the conversion of nearly every student in the school. In some terms this has been the case without exception, and in others there have not been more than two or three exceptions. Business men have brought their children from Newcastle to our school in Avondale, so that they would not be tempted as they would be in the public schools, which they declared were corrupted. Our schools should be located away from the cities, on a large tract of land, so that the students will have opportunity to do manual work. They should have opportunity to learn lessons from the objects which Christ used in the inculcation of truth. He pointed to the birds, to the flowers, to the sower and the reaper.

"In schools of this kind not only are the minds of the students benefited, but their physical powers are strengthened. All portions of the body are exercised. The education of mind and body is equalized. The body needs a great deal more care than it gets. There are men here who are suffering, O so much, because they are not faithful stewards of their bodies. God wants you to use every means in your power to care for the wonderful machinery which he has given you. Let no part of it rust from inaction" (GCB April 14, 1901).

Emmanuel Missionary College, MI - Est. 1901
(now Andrews University)

"The good hand of the Lord has been with our people in the selection of a good place to locate the school. This place corresponds to the representation given me as to where the school should be located. It is away from the cities, and there is an abundance of land for agricultural purposes, and room so that houses will not need to be built one close to another. There is plenty of ground where students shall be educated to cultivate the land. 'Ye are God's husbandry; ye are God's building'" (Lt186-1901).

"I thank the Lord that the brethren heeded the instruction given to them, and that they carried forth His work in simplicity and meekness, and yet intelligently. The Lord is qualifying them to teach the lessons He has given in His Word by object lessons from nature. This is the grandest, the most helpful, all-around education that the youth can have. Cultivating the soil, planting and caring for trees, sowing seed and watching its growth—this work teaches precious lessons. Nature is an expositor of the Word of the living God. But only through Christ does creation answer the highest purpose of the Creator. The Saviour has wonderful revelations for all who will walk humbly with God. Under the discipline and training of the higher teaching, they will behold wondrous things out of His law.

"In establishing schools, enough land should be secured to give the students opportunity to gain a knowledge of agriculture. If it is necessary to curtail the expense anywhere, let it be on the buildings. There should be no failure to secure land; for from the cultivation of the soil, the students are to learn lessons illustrating the truths of the word of God, truths that will help them to understand the work of the Creator" (Ms98-1902).

"The Lord instructed me that some connected with the institution would not see the necessity of uniting agricultural work with the instruction given in the school. In all our educational institutions, physical and mental work should have been combined. In vigorous physical exercise, the animal passions find a healthy outlet and are kept in proper bounds. Healthful exercise in the open air will strengthen the muscles, encourage a proper circulation of blood, help to preserve the body from disease, and will be a great help in spirituality. For many years it has been presented to me that teachers and students should unite in this work. This was done anciently in the schools of the prophets" (Ms40-1903).

"The Lord was in this school's being established. The Lord helped these brethren as they progressed with their school, and as they were teaching the very principles that were taught in the schools of the prophets. Do you think in the schools of the prophets they went back to all those books that are brought into the school to give an education? Do you think they took the study books that were in the common schools? No, No! What were they taught? To have a knowledge of Jesus Christ. If they have a practical knowledge of Jesus Christ, let me tell you, they understand that they must be partakers of the divine nature in order to escape corruption that is in the world through lust, and come out of the cities. It is the very thing to do today. Get them out of the cities into the rural places, where they may be educated in agriculture and the various lines of business and trade. Do you suppose that when the times are growing worse and worse that you will all be left together here in one company? No, we shall be scattered. If those who are helping educate in this place shall give the right kind of education, these students will be qualified to go out into new places and begin with ABC work to educate others. As they commence, the Holy Spirit of God will stand by their side" (SpM 357 [extracts from talks given at the Lake Union Conference, June 1904]).

Madison School, TN - Est. 1904

"The plan upon which our brethren propose to work is to select some of the best and most substantial young men and women from Berrien Springs, and other places in the North, who believe that God has called them to the work in the South, and give them a brief training as teachers. Thorough instruction will be given in Bible study, physiology, the history of our message; and special instruction will be given regarding the cultivation of the land. It is hoped that many of these students will eventually connect with schools in various places in the South. In connection with these schools there will be land that will be cultivated by teachers and students, and the proceeds from this work will be used for the support of the schools" (Lt215-1904).

"The Madison school farm is to be an object lesson for the southern field. It is in an excellent location and fully as near Nashville as it should be" (Lt352-1906).

"The Lord has given to the southern field object lessons of different kinds. The education being given to the students at Madison which trains the youth to build, to cultivate the land, and to care for cattle and poultry, will be of great advantage to them in the future. There is no better way of keeping the body in health than to follow the plan of training that the Madison school is carrying out. This is the same kind of work as we were instructed to do when we purchased the land for our school in Australia. The students had their hours for study and their hours for work on the land. They were taught to fell trees, to plant orchards, to cultivate the soil, and to erect buildings, and this training was a blessing to all who engaged in it....

"The work that the laborers have accomplished at Madison has done more to give a correct knowledge of what an all-round education means than any other school that has been established by Seventh-day Adventists in America. The Lord has given these teachers in the South an education that is of highest value, and it is a training that God would be pleased to have all our youth receive.

> *"The work... at Madison has done more to give a correct knowledge of what an all-round education means than any other other school that has been established by Seventh-day Adventists in America."*

"The close confinement of students to mental work has cost the life of many precious youth. The Madison school, in its system of education, is showing that mental and physical powers, brain and muscle, must be equally taxed. The example that it has given in this respect is one that it would be well for all who engage in school work to emulate. If the physical and mental powers were equally taxed, there would be in our world far less of corruption of mind and far less feebleness of health" (Lt168-1908).

"Throughout the southern field, just such object lessons [as Madison] are needed. Such schools would prove of the highest advantage to the people, demonstrating that education embraces more than the mere study of books, that it also includes useful employment in any line. And one of the most useful employments for the people of the South is the cultivation of the land that has run to waste for lack of care and attention. The exercise of the muscles and the reason in the performance of physical labor is to be combined with the exercise of the mental powers in the study of books. This is the kind of education that will recommend the students if they should be called to work in foreign countries" (Lt382-1908).

Misc. Specific Schools
"We knew that the school must be established away from the city, and that we must have land, so that the students could have opportunity to gain a knowledge of agriculture, and opportunity also to be self-supporting. The light given me is that we are to take our children away from the congested cities, and do all in our power to prepare them for the future life. The Fernando [CA] school is situated in an orange district. On every hand are to be seen beautiful orange groves" (Lt211-1902).

"A few days ago I had the privilege of seeing the buildings and the surroundings of the Fernando school. My time was very limited, but I was thankful for the opportunity of visiting the school-grounds. I am glad that you are several miles away from the city of Los Angeles. You have good buildings, and are in a favorable place for school work. I greatly desire that you shall make a right beginning. In planning for the erection of cottages for our brethren and sisters who may move there, be careful not to allow buildings to be put up too near the school property. Try to secure the land lying near the school, so that it will be impossible for houses to be built close to the campus. The land may be used for agricultural purposes. Later on, you may find it advisable to introduce various trades for the employment and training of the students; but at present about all that you can do is to teach them how to cultivate the land, so that it shall yield its fruit.

"The question has been asked, 'What shall we teach in the Fernando school?' Teach the very simplest lessons. You should not make a great parade before the world, showing what you expect to do, as if you were planning to do something wonderful. No, indeed. Take hold of this school with meekness. Tell your brethren and friends that you are planning to conduct an industrial school, a school in which practical instruction in agriculture and various trades will be connected with instruction in book learning. Boast neither of the branches of study you expect to teach nor of the industrial work you hope to do; but tell every one who inquires that you intend to do the best you can to give your students a physical, mental, and spiritual training that will fit them for usefulness in this life, and prepare them for the future, immortal life" (Ms54-1903).

"On Sunday we were taken to see the different lines of work that are being carried on by our people in Graysville [TN]. We went over the school buildings, and then we visited the twenty-five-acre farm on the hill, which is largely planted out to peaches. The young trees looks [sic] thrifty. After looking at this, we went to see the four-hundred-acre farm which has recently been acquired by the Conference and has been leased to the school. On this farm we saw large fields of corn being cultivated by the students, broad pasture land, and on the hill thirty acres of strawberries" (Lt215-1904).

"I am deeply interested in the work that is being done here [Hillcrest School, Nashville, TN], because special light has been given me regarding the neglect there has been to take up the work you are doing. I have specified in my writings what this work is. I have tried again and again to impress its importance on the minds of the people. I shall still talk of it wherever I go.

"You are not working alone. When you are tempted to become discouraged, remember this: Angels of God are right around you. They will minister to the very ground and the earth, causing it to give forth its treasures.

"Angels of God are right around you. They will minister to the very ground and the earth, causing it to give forth its treasures."

"This is the instruction I am trying to give to our people. I want them to understand what could be accomplished if we would work the will of the Lord. It is the Lord who has given the instruction. Let us follow His directions" (Ms13, 1909).

"There has been some delay in getting the title to the Buena Vista property [CA]. We are looking forward to having the matter settled soon. This is an excellent site for a school. As soon as I saw it I was sure that it would make an ideal place for the carrying on of our educational work, for we can combine physical work on the farm with the study of books. Here the students can be taught to build and to engage in many useful lines of labor, as the students at Madison are being taught to do. There should also be sanitarium facilities in connection with the school, for I have been shown that where we have a training school, we should have a sanitarium where the students can receive instruction in caring for the sick and suffering" (Lt18-1909).

The South
"Those who love Christ will do the works of Christ. They will go forth to seek and to save that which was lost. They will not shun those who are despised, and turn aside from the colored race. They will teach them how to read and how to perform manual labor, educating them to till the soil and to follow trades of various kinds. They will put forth painstaking efforts to develop the capabilities of the people" (RH January 14, 1896).

"Schools are to be established away from the cities, in places where plenty of land can be obtained. Thus the students can be given opportunity to help to support themselves while in schools, and at the same time they learn the valuable lessons taught by the cultivation of the soil. With the schools are to be connected various other industries....

"We must provide greater facilities for the education and training of the youth, both white and colored. We are to establish schools away from the cities, where the youth can learn to cultivate the soil, and thus help to make themselves and the school self-supporting.... In connection with these schools work is to be done in mechanical and agricultural lines. All the different lines of work that the situation of the place will warrant are to be brought in.

"Carpentering, blacksmithing, agriculture, the best way to make the most of what the earth produces—all these things are part of the education to be given to the youth....

"There are places where the work has been started, that seem unprofitable. But let not these places be abandoned. Let earnest, diligent efforts be put forth to make the work in them a success. Some places are specially adapted for the cultivation of fruit. And in planting, cultivating, and pruning fruit trees, students may learn precious spiritual lessons. Other places may be adapted for the cultivation of grains and vegetables" (Lt25-1902).

"Special efforts should be put forth to perfect the work in the places of the South where schools have been established—Graysville [TN], Huntsville [AL], and Hildebran [NC]. The schools are to be sustained by the starting of various industries.

"The time will come when those who embrace the truth in the cities will have to take their families away from the cities, and these industries will help to provide them with homes and employment....

"In establishing schools, the important thing is to find a location where industries can be started that will enable the students to be self-supporting. The work should be carried on with as little outlay of means as possible. In connection with a school there should be enough land to raise sufficient crops for the school consumption, and also some to sell for the benefit of the school.

"Nashville, Graysville, Huntsville, and Hildebran have been presented to me as places favorable for raising crops for the use of the schools and for marketing....

"The students should learn to cultivate the soil and to raise whatever the land will produce. No one can tell what can be done with the soil till he has experimented—planting seeds and setting out fruit trees and vines.

"The young men attending our schools should be taught how to build houses plainly and inexpensively, yet substantially. They are to be taught that God will not accept any haphazard, slipshod work. From whatever work they do—building, sowing, planting, or reaping, they are to learn the lesson, 'Ye are God's husbandry; ye are God's building.' They are to learn that which will prepare them to act their part in teaching others trades" (Lt27-1902).

[Alternate version] "In establishing schools, one important point is to secure land sufficient for the carrying forward of industries that will enable the students to be self-supporting. There should be land sufficient for the raising of the fruit and vegetables required by the school, and also some for sale. Agriculture should be made a financial benefit to the school.

"Nashville, Graysville, Huntsville, and Hildebran have been presented to me as places favorable for the raising of crops for the use of the school, and for marketing....

"The young men should learn to cultivate the soil, and to raise whatever the land will produce. No one can tell what can be done with the soil until he has studied, planned, and experimented" (PH151 76, 1903).

"I have spent one-half hour talking with two of our brethren in regard to their disposing of their property and removing their families to the southern field for the purpose of doing missionary work, having a school, and preparing their children to work in various lines in the missionary work, such as cultivating farms, building humble homes, and teaching the people the art of building and the art of cultivating the soil. The time will come that all who live upon the earth will need to understand the cultivating of the land and the building of houses and varied kinds of business. We tried to tell them that the Lord is calling for talent to be brought into the southern field, and act in various lines of education. Shall it be that we shall go into the southern field and bear the truth to those who have not heard the truth? This class must not be discouraged. The youth educated in our large cities are in great danger because they are surrounded with every kind of objectionable influence, for the world is becoming as it was in the days of Noah" (Ms126-1908).

FOR ADDITIONAL READING

Ms8a-1894 (also re-published in SpTEd, chapter 14 and FE chapter 41). I believe this to be Mrs. White's seminal work on agriculture/manual labor and it deserves to be read in its entirety.

Ed, chapter on "Manual Training," pp. 214–222.

6T Section 3.

Agriculture and Our Health Care Institutions

"I saw the beneficial influence of outdoor labor upon those of feeble vitality and depressed circulation, especially upon women who have induced these conditions by too much confinement indoors. Their blood has become impure for want of fresh air and exercise. Instead of amusements to keep these persons indoors, care should be taken to provide outdoor attractions. I saw there should be connected with the Institute ample grounds, beautified with flowers and planted with vegetables and fruits. Here the feeble could find work, appropriate to their sex and condition, at suitable hours. These grounds should be under the care of an experienced gardener to direct all in a tasteful, orderly manner" (1T 562, 1868).

"Invalids should have out-door exercise. That class of invalids, who have made themselves such by sedentary habits, or constant mental labor, should have a change. It is bad counsel that tells these persons to refrain from physical exercise. The brain-weary ones should, in a great degree, let the mental powers rest, while they, and also those whose habits of life have been sedentary, should stir the physical energies. A part of the prescription for every such patient should be light physical labor, pleasant employment out of doors.

"To merely engage in simple plays for amusement, cannot satisfy the conscientious, but will leave the impression upon the mind of the invalid that his life is useless. And if his life has been active, and he has taken pleasure in doing good, the influence of such amusements upon him will be bad. Let this class of sufferers have pleasant employment out of doors, suited to their several conditions, both as to the nature of the work, and the time they should be engaged in it. Let those who are able to take a light, well-polished hoe, and for a suitable number of hours, or minutes, institute a war of extermination upon unwelcome weeds among vegetables and small fruits. Let others, more feeble, use the garden trowel, rake, or hoe, a few moments each day among the plants and flowers, and let them feel that every weed they pull up they do some good. What if the sun does burn the face and hands brown? The sun and the air will do them more good than water baths can do without these blessings.

"Some who have broken down because of too much brain-labor, and not enough physical exercise, feel disinclined to enjoy out-door exercise. If they cease brain-work, they do not wish to do anything. And it is difficult for these to recover health, for the reason that it is nearly impossible to control their minds. Their active minds, when not otherwise engaged, will be dwelling upon themselves. The imagination is diseased, and they often think themselves in a deplorable condition when they are not. Give such suitable employment, and let them feel that their lives are not useless, but that they are doing some good, although it be but little, and they will be far less inclined to dwell upon themselves. Pleasing out-door labor is the grand remedy for such. Let their time be divided. Let them spend a portion of each day in pleasant in-door occupations, a portion out in the air and sunshine, working among vegetables, fruits, flowers and plants, and a portion in rest. This doing system is a great blessing to both body and mind. While doing something, the mind is diverted from self, and has something to do besides chasing after symptoms, aches and pains. And physical exercise will bring into use muscles and nerves that have been inactive, and have become weak for want of use. As these invalids exercise and strengthen their feeble, flabby muscles, the brain becomes less inclined to wearing activity. The work now becomes better divided between the organs of the system.

"I have noticed that those who have broken down because of too much brain labor, as they commence to improve, feel a special desire to engage in mental labor. They seem anxious to engage again in head-work. If such could be made to see that this is the wrong kind of employment; that healthful labor in the open air and in household duties, is what they need to give firmness to the muscles and healthful tone to the mind, they would no longer be anxious for that kind of labor which wearies the brain and gives no strength to the muscles or nerves of the body" (HR July 1, 1868).

"Live, dear invalid friends, while you do live, and train yourselves to shed fragrance like the fresh flowers. If you are burdened and weary, you need not curl up like leaves upon a withered branch. Cheerfulness and a clear conscience are better than drugs, and will be an effective agent in your restoration to health. In order for you to be cheerful, you should have exercise. You should have something useful to do. Invalid sisters should have something to call them out of doors, to work in the ground. This was the employment given by God to our first parents. God knew that employment was necessary to happiness. You should have a spot of ground to claim as yours, to tend and cultivate. You may have a pride in keeping out every weed, and may watch with interest the beautiful development of every leaf and opening bud and flower, and be charmed with the miracles of God seen in nature. As you view the shrubs and flowers, remember God loves the beautiful in nature. As you watch the harmonious colors of the various beautiful-tinted flowers of June, bear in mind that God loves the beautiful in human nature formed in his image. A pure, harmonious character, a sunny temper, reflecting light and cheerfulness, glorifies God, and benefits humanity. Inspiration tells us that a meek and quiet spirit in the sight of God is of great price" (HR June 1, 1871).

"Sanitariums that are erected for consumptive patients should be placed some distance out of the city, where there is plenty of open space, a clear stream, and land which can be cultivated. Then the patients can be drawn out into the fresh air, while those who are strong can cultivate the soil. The institution built for consumptives which has not these accompaniments cannot benefit the patients. Such an institution Seventh-day Adventists are at the present time unable to maintain" (Ms89-1899).

"The surroundings of a sanitarium should be as attractive as possible. Out-of-door life is a means of gaining health and happiness…. In flower garden and orchard, the sick will find health, cheerfulness, and happy thoughts" (Ms43-1902).

"Encourage the patients to be much in the open air. Devise plans to keep them out of doors, where, through nature, they can commune with God. Locate sanitariums on extensive tracts of land, where, in the cultivation of the soil, patients can have opportunity for healthful, outdoor exercise. Such exercise, combined with hygienic treatment, will work miracles in restoring and invigorating the diseased body and refreshing the worn and weary mind. Amid conditions so favorable the patients will not require so much care as if confined in a sanitarium in the city. Nor will they in the country be so much inclined to discontentment and repining. They will be ready to learn lessons in regard to the love of God, ready to acknowledge that He who cares so wonderfully for the birds and the flowers will care for the creatures formed in His own image. Thus opportunity is given physicians and helpers to reach souls, uplifting the God of nature before those who are seeking restoration to health.

"In the night season I was given a view of a sanitarium in the country. The institution was not large, but it was complete. It was surrounded by beautiful trees and shrubbery, beyond which were orchards and groves. Connected with the place were gardens, in which the lady patients, when they chose, could cultivate flowers of every description, each patient selecting a special plot for which to care. Outdoor exercise in these gardens was prescribed as a part of the regular treatment.

"Scene after scene passed before me. In one scene a number of suffering patients had just come to one of our country sanitariums. In another I saw the same company; but, oh, how transformed their appearance! Disease had gone, the skin was clear, the countenance joyful; body and mind seemed animated with new life....

"Light has been given me that in medical missionary work we have lost great advantages by failing to realize the need of a change in our plans in regard to the location of sanitariums. It is the Lord's will that these institutions shall be established outside the city. They should be situated in the country, in the midst of surroundings as attractive as possible. In nature—the Lord's garden—the sick will always find something to divert their attention from themselves and lift their thoughts to God.

> *"In nature—the Lord's garden—the sick will always find something to divert their attention from themselves and lift their thoughts to God."*

"I have been instructed that the sick should be cared for away from the bustle of the cities, away from the noise of streetcars and the continual rattling of carts and carriages. People who come to our sanitariums from country homes will appreciate a quiet place; and in retirement patients will be more readily influenced by the Spirit of God.

"The Garden of Eden, the home of our first parents, was exceedingly beautiful. Graceful shrubs and delicate flowers greeted the eye at every turn. In the garden were trees of every variety, many of them laden with fragrant and delicious fruit. On their branches the birds caroled their songs of praise. Adam and Eve, in their untainted purity, delighted in the sights and sounds of Eden. And today, although sin has cast its shadow over the earth, God desires His children to find delight in the works of His hands. To locate our sanitariums amidst the scenes of nature would be to follow God's plan; and the more closely this plan is followed, the more wonderfully will He work to restore suffering humanity. For our educational and medical institutions, places should be chosen where, away from the dark clouds of sin that hang over the great cities, the Sun of Righteousness can arise, 'with healing in His wings.' Malachi 4:2.

"Let the leaders in our work instruct the people that sanitariums should be established in the midst of the most pleasant surroundings, in places not disturbed by the turmoil of the city, places where by wise instruction the thoughts of the patients can be bound up with the thoughts of God. Again and again I have described such places; but it seems that there has been no ear to hear. Recently in a most clear and convincing manner the advantage of establishing our institutions, especially our sanitariums and schools, outside the cities was presented to me.

"Why are our physicians so eager to be located in the cities? The very atmosphere of the cities is polluted. In them, patients who have unnatural appetites to overcome cannot be properly guarded. To patients who are victims of strong drink, the saloons of a city are a continual temptation. To place our sanitariums where they are surrounded by ungodliness is to counterwork the efforts made to restore the patients to health....

"Why deprive patients of the health-restoring blessing to be found in outdoor life? I have been instructed that as the sick are encouraged to leave their rooms and spend time in the open air, cultivating flowers, or doing some other light, pleasant work, their minds will be called from self to something more health-giving. Exercise in the open air should be prescribed as a beneficial, life-giving necessity. The longer patients can be kept out of doors the less care will they require. The more cheerful their surroundings, the more hopeful will they be. Surround them with the beautiful things of nature; place them where they can see the flowers growing and hear the birds singing, and their hearts will break into song in harmony with the song of the birds. Shut them in rooms, and, be these rooms ever so elegantly furnished, they will grow fretful and gloomy. Give them the blessing of outdoor life; thus their souls will be uplifted. Relief will come to body and mind....

"There was among us One who presented this matter very clearly and with the utmost simplicity. He told us that it would be a mistake to establish a sanitarium within the city limits. A sanitarium should have the advantage of plenty of land, so that the invalids can work in the open air. For nervous, gloomy, feeble patients, outdoor work is invaluable. Let them have flower beds to care for. In the use of rake and hoe and spade they will find relief for many of their maladies. Idleness is the cause of many diseases.

"Life in the open air is good for body and mind. It is God's medicine for the restoration of health. Pure air, good water, sunshine, the beautiful surroundings of nature—these are His means for restoring the sick to health in natural ways. To the sick it is worth more than silver or gold to lie in the sunshine or in the shade of the trees.

"In the country our sanitariums can be surrounded by flowers and trees, orchards and vineyards. Here it is easy for physicians and nurses to draw from the things of nature lessons teaching of God. Let them point the patients to Him whose hand has made the lofty trees, the springing grass, and the beautiful flowers, encouraging them to see in every opening bud and blossoming flower an expression of His love for His children" (7T 78–85, 1902).

"This morning Sara and I rode down to see Sister Hizerman. I wish that I had time to give you a full account of our conversation with her. She told me that she used to be an invalid, sick and suffering. At that time they had no home of their own. They purchased the place on which they are now living. The ground is very good, but the house is rather old. While Brother Hizerman worked at his trade, Sister Hizerman began to cultivate the garden connected with the house. She says that at first she was able to work only for a short time, and then her back would ache so severely that she would be obliged to go into the house and lie down. But gradually she gained in health and strength, and now she can work for a long time without getting tired. She does most of the gardening, and this morning she took pride in showing us her growing crops. Her hands are hard, but her health is greatly improved. She says that in the past she has spent much time in sanitariums, but that all the treatment she received did not do her so much good as her work in the open air has done her. The physical exercise was just what she needed....

"The benefit that Sister Hizerman's work in the garden has been to her is a lesson for us all. It shows what such work would accomplish for the patients at our sanitariums. It would work a cure without drugs. O how many invalids might be healed if the Lord's methods were followed. Weak and trembling, Sister Hizerman began her work, and now she is strong and well. Her outdoor exercise has surrounded her with an atmosphere of serenity. She has indeed been greatly blessed. She is full of peace and happiness. Her weakness has gone. The satisfaction of seeing what she could do has strengthened her purpose to do more" (Lt138-1903).

"I have received much instruction regarding the location of sanitariums. They should be a few miles distant from the large cities, and land should be secured in connection with them. Fruit and vegetables should be cultivated, and the patients should be encouraged to take up outdoor work. Many who are suffering from pulmonary disease might be cured if they would live in a climate where they could be out-of-doors most of the year. Many who have died of consumption might have lived if they had breathed more pure air. Fresh outdoor air is as healing as medicine, and leaves no injurious after effects" (Ms115-1903).

"The Lord permitted fire to consume the principal buildings of the Review and Herald and the Sanitarium and thus removed the greatest objection raised to moving out of Battle Creek. It was His design, not that one large sanitarium should be rebuilt, but that plants should be made in several places. These smaller sanitariums should have been established where they could have the benefit and advantage of land for agricultural purposes. It is God's plan that agriculture shall be carried on in connection with our sanitariums and schools. Our youth need the education to be gained from this line of work. It is well, and more than well—it is essential—that efforts be made to carry out the Lord's plan in this respect" (Ms129-1903).

> *"It is God's plan that agriculture shall be carried on in connection with our sanitariums and schools.... It is well, and more than well—it is essential—that efforts be made to carry out the Lord's plan in this respect."*

"Our sanitariums should not be situated in or near any city. And it is most important that in connection with them land be secured, that homes may be provided for those who help in the institution, and also that facilities for outdoor work be provided for the patients.... Let men and women work in field and orchard and garden. This will bring health and strength to nerve and muscle. Living indoors and cherishing invalidism is a very poor business. If those who are sick will give nerves and muscles and sinews proper exercise in the open air, their health will be renewed....

"If those who are sick would exercise their muscles daily, women as well as men, in outdoor work, using brain, bone, and muscle proportionately, weakness and languor would disappear. Health would take the place of disease, and strength the place of feebleness....

"A few words more in regard to the location of our sanitariums. Never, never should these institutions be established in the cities. They should be established in the country, amidst pleasant surroundings, and in connection with plenty of land. This is a positive necessity. Flower and vegetable gardens and orchards will be found to be health-giving agencies in the successful treatment of the sick. Many who come to our sanitariums to receive the benefit of these advantages will be blessed with improved health. So interested will they become in the work given them to do that they will forget their aches and pains....

"Land we must have, that the patients may be provided with out-door employment" (Lt5-1904).

"The buildings secured for this work should be out of the cities, in the country, so that the sick may have the benefit of outdoor life. By the beauty of flower and field, their minds will be diverted from themselves, from their aches and pains, and they will be led to look from nature to the God of nature, who has provided so abundantly the beauties of the natural world. The convalescent can lie in the shade of the trees, and those who are stronger can, if they wish, work among the flowers, doing just a little at first, and increasing their efforts as they grow stronger. Working in the garden, gathering flowers and fruit, listening to the birds praising God, the patients will be wonderfully blessed. Angels of God will draw near to them. They will forget their sorrows. Melancholy and depression will leave them. The fresh air and sunshine, and the exercise taken, will bring them life and vitality. The wearied brain and nerves will find relief. Good treatment and a wholesome diet will build them up and strengthen them. They will feel no need for health-destroying drugs or for intoxicating drink" (Lt147-1904).

"Institutions for the care of the sick would be far more successful if they could be established away from the cities. And so far as possible, all who are seeking to recover health should place themselves amid country surroundings where they can have the benefit of outdoor life....

"Plans should be devised for keeping patients out of doors. For those who are able to work, let some pleasant, easy employment be provided.

Show them how agreeable and helpful this outdoor work is. Encourage them to breathe the fresh air. Teach them to breathe deeply, and in breathing and speaking to exercise the abdominal muscles. This is an education that will be invaluable to them.

"Exercise in the open air should be prescribed as a life-giving necessity. And for such exercises there is nothing better than the cultivation of the soil. Let patients have flower beds to care for, or work to do in the orchard or vegetable garden. As they are encouraged to leave their rooms and spend time in the open air, cultivating flowers or doing some other light, pleasant work, their attention will be diverted from themselves and their sufferings.

"The more the patient can be kept out of doors, the less care will he require. The more cheerful his surroundings, the more helpful will he be. Shut up in the house, be it ever so elegantly furnished, he will grow fretful and gloomy. Surround him with the beautiful things of nature; place him where he can see the flowers growing and hear the birds singing, and his heart will break into song in harmony with the songs of the birds. Relief will come to body and mind. The intellect will be awakened, the imagination quickened, and the mind prepared to appreciate the beauty of God's word.

"In nature may always be found something to divert the attention of the sick from themselves and direct their thoughts to God. Surrounded by His wonderful works, their minds are uplifted from the things that are seen to the things that are unseen. The beauty of nature leads them to think of the heavenly home, where there will be nothing to mar the loveliness, nothing to taint or destroy, nothing to cause disease or death.

"Let physicians and nurses draw from the things of nature, lessons teaching of God. Let them point the patients to Him whose hand has made the lofty trees, the grass, and the flowers, encouraging them to see in every bud and flower an expression of His love for His children. He who cares for the birds and the flowers will care for the beings formed in His own image.

"Out of doors, amid the things that God has made, breathing the fresh, health-giving air, the sick can best be told of the new life in Christ. Here God's word can be read. Here the light of Christ's righteousness can shine into hearts darkened by sin" (MH 263–266, 1905).

"I have written several times regarding the necessity of our sanitariums being established in suitable places, where there is an abundance of land, so that the patients can spend as much time as possible out of doors. If possible, the buildings should be surrounded with pleasant grounds, beautified with flowers and shade-trees, under which, in wheel-chairs, on their cots, or on comfortable seats, the patients can listen to the music of the birds. Those who are well enough should be encouraged to cultivate flowers and to engage in other outdoor exercise that will take their minds off themselves" (Lt295-1905).

"The land [at Loma Linda, CA] is well cultivated and will furnish much fruit and many vegetables for the institutions. Fifteen acres of the valley land are in alfalfa hay. Eight acres of the hill are in apricots, plums, and lemons. The acres are in good-bearing orange orchard. Many acres of land round the cottages and the main building are laid out in lawns, drives, and walks.

"There are horses and carriages, cows and poultry, farming implements and wagons. The buildings and grounds are abundantly supplied with excellent water" (Lt237-1905).

"The character of the buildings, the terraced hill, covered by graceful pepper trees, the profusion of flowers and shrubs, the tall shade trees, the orchards and fields,—all combine to make this place meet fully the descriptions that I have given in the past of the place presented to me as the most perfect for sanitarium work. Everything at Loma Linda is fresh, wholesome, and attractive. The patients could live out of doors a large part of the time. The land will serve as a school for the education of patients. By outdoor exercise and working in the soil, men and women will regain their health. Rational methods for the cure of disease will be used in a variety of ways. Drugs will be discarded.

"Out of the cities, has been my constant advice. But it has taken years for our people to become aroused to an understanding of the situation. It has taken years for them to realize that the Lord would have them leave the cities and do their work in the quiet of the country, away from the turmoil and noise and confusion. We are thankful to God for Loma Linda. It is one of the best locations for sanitarium work that I have ever seen. At this place the sick can be given every natural advantage for regaining health and strength" (SpTB03b 14, 1905).

"While at Loma Linda we were taken by Brother Burden to view the garden. This land is being wisely cultivated, and it is yielding its treasures. In the last year the garden has brought in $600 in profits, and Brother

Burden expressed his conviction that this would continue to improve. We saw large patches of melons, strawberries, asparagus, tomatoes, and corn. Some of these fruits and vegetables are sold in the neighboring town, but the larger portion is used to supply the sanitarium tables" (Lt258-1908).

"At Loma Linda I found that great advancement had been made. I was taken in an easy carriage over a large part of the farm, and Elder Burden told of the success that had attended their orchard, farm, and garden enterprises. It was a great pleasure to see the thrifty fruit trees and the prosperous garden. The land had been diligently and faithfully cultivated, and it is yielding its treasure for the support of the sanitarium" (Lt268-1908).

"Let not our brethren feel it their duty to restrict the investment of means where it is needed. It is in the Lord's order that the sanitarium [in Lafayette, IN] has been secured. More land should have been purchased, and if possible, this should be done now. The grounds around a sanitarium should not be restricted. Provision should be made for the raising of fruit and vegetables, and it should not be made possible for buildings of an objectionable character to be erected near our institutions.

"The plan of having our sanitariums out of the cities is born of the Lord. This should be borne in mind, and sufficient land should be secured to raise fruit and vegetables. It will be a boon to the sick and to the helpers to be given outdoor work on the land. Many of our own workers have broken down in health through excessive mental taxation without the balance of physical exercise" (RH December 23, 1909).

FOR ADDITIONAL READING

7T, Section 2, "Our Sanitarium Work," pp. 76–87

MH, chapter 19, "In Contact With Nature," pp. 261–268

Agriculture for Ministers and Other Gospel Workers

"God knows with what fidelity and spirit of consecration everyone fulfills his mission. There is no place for the slothful in this great work, no place for the self-indulgent or those who are incapable of making life a success in any calling, no place for halfhearted men who are not fervent in spirit, willing to endure hardness, opposition, reproach, or death for Christ's sake. The Christian ministry is no place for drones. There is a class of men attempting to preach who are slipshod, careless, and irreverent. They would better be tilling the soil than teaching the sacred truth of God" (5T 582, 1889).

"Those who are engaged in constant mental labor, whether in study or preaching, need rest and change. The earnest student is constantly taxing the brain, too often while neglecting physical exercise, and as the result the bodily powers are enfeebled, and mental effort is restricted. Thus the student fails of accomplishing the very work that he might have done, had he labored wisely.

"If they worked intelligently, giving both mind and body a due share of exercise, ministers would not so readily succumb to disease. If all our workers were so situated that they could spend a few hours each day in out-door labor, and felt free to do this, it would be a blessing to them; they would be able to discharge more successfully the duties of their calling. If they have not time for complete relaxation, they could be planning and praying while at work with their hands, and could return to their labor refreshed in body and spirit.

"Some of our ministers feel that they must every day perform some labor that they can report to the Conference. And as the result of trying to do this, their efforts are too often weak and inefficient. They should have periods of rest, of entire freedom from taxing labor. But these cannot take the place of daily physical exercise.

"Brethren, when you take time to cultivate your garden, thus gaining the exercise needed to keep the system in good working order, you are just as much doing the work of God as in holding meetings. God is our Father, he loves us, and he does not require any of his servants to abuse their bodies" (GW92 173, 174, 1892).

> *"Brethren, when you take time to cultivate your garden... you are just as much doing the work of God as in holding meetings."*

"How many useful and honored workers in God's cause have received a training amid the humble duties of the most lowly positions in life. Moses was the prospective ruler of Egypt, but God could not take him from the king's court to do the work appointed him. Only when he had been for forty years a faithful shepherd was he sent to be the deliverer of his people. Gideon was taken from the threshing of wheat to be the instrument in the hands of God for delivering the armies of Israel. Elisha was called to leave the plow and do the bidding of God. Amos was husbandman, a tiller of the soil, when God gave him a message to proclaim.

"These lessons should be kept in view by those who have to do with the training of workers for the cause of God. All who become co-workers with Christ will have a great deal of hard, uncongenial labor to perform, and their lessons of instruction should be wisely chosen, and adapted to their peculiarities of character, and the work which they are to pursue" (GW92 316, 317, 1892).

"It would be well if ministers who labor in word or doctrine could enter the fields and spend some portion of the day in physical exercise with the students [at our schools]. They could do as Christ did in giving lessons from nature to illustrate Bible truth" (Ms8a-1894).

"Many errors are entertained by men in their vocations. They overestimate their capabilities, and in test and trial reveal that they need a different kind of experience than they have had in order to be a laborer together with Christ. The men who do not see their need of serving God in little things, doing humble work, give unmistakable evidence that they are not fitted to serve in larger things. In overlooking the humble service as non-essential, they bear testimony that they cannot be trusted with larger responsibilities.

"The idea which prevails in some minds, and which it is difficult to change, an idea which they have permitted to be unconsciously woven into their experience, is that a certain position of gentility and dignity must be maintained or their influence will be marred in their work of preaching. But when these learn to minister, they will know that humble, active service means to interest themselves in the duties of everyday life, and [to] obtain the education essential to do the ordinary duties of life in any small vocation—it may be in tilling the soil, in following the plough, in sowing or in reaping. Service to God means work in different lines. It is not merely to study and contemplate and preach, and allow the hands to remain idle. That religion is spurious which does not reveal itself in labor in Christ's lines.

"There is to be no neglect or low estimate of the humble every day duties of life. True conversion to God will act as leaven in every phase of duty in the relationships of life. Then if the Lord sees us faithful in that which is least, diligent and persevering in the use of our physical powers, doing with our hands that which some one must do, He will say, 'Come up higher. You may be entrusted with greater responsibilities.' You are to be an educator of the youth who have perverted ideas of the religion of usefulness and duty. They fail to learn the ennobling lessons that will make a man an all-round character in the sight of God, and to be just as useful in the field, in planting, in sowing, in harvesting, in the various duties of the home guard, as in the field of conflict. Such characters will be qualified to discern the deep, hidden treasures of the Word of God" (Lt64-1897).

"If a minister, during his leisure time, engages in labor in his orchard or garden, shall he deduct that time from his salary? Certainly not, any more than he should put in his time when he is called to work over hours in ministerial labor.... There are hours in the day that call for severe taxation, for which the minister receives no extra salary, and if he chooses to chop wood several hours a day, or work in his garden, it is as much his privilege to do this as to preach. A minister cannot always be preaching and visiting, for this is exhaustive work.

"The light given me is that if our ministers would do more physical labor, they would reap blessings healthwise....

"If these men could go aside and rest a while, engaging in physical labor, it would be a great relief and blessing.... It is a positive necessity to physical health and mental clearness to do some manual work during the day" (Lt168-1899).

"If you go out as a canvasser, and meet a man toiling in the field, join him in labor. Take the hoe, or whatever instrument he may be using, and work by his side while you are talking with him. Tell him that you know he is busy, and that you have no desire to hinder him. Let me assure you that the sermon you preach with the hoe will be in harmony with the sermon which you preach with your tongue; and the two, together, have a power which words alone could never have" (Ms126-1902).

"Those who go forth from our schools to engage in mission work will have need of an experience in the cultivation of the soil and in other lines of manual labor. They should receive a training that will fit them to take hold of any line of work in the fields to which they shall be called. No work will be more effectual than that done by those who, having obtained and education in practical life, go forth prepared to instruct as they have been instructed" (RH October 24, 1907).

"The usefulness learned on the school farm is the very education that is most essential for those who go out as missionaries to many foreign fields. If this training is given with the glory of God in view, great results will be seen. No work will be more effectual than that done by those who, having obtained an education in practical life, go forth to mission fields with the message of truth, prepared to instruct as they have been instructed. The knowledge they have obtained in the tilling of the soil, in the erection of buildings, and in other lines of manual work, and which they carry with them to their field of labor, will make them a blessing even in heathen lands" (RH February 6, 1908).

> *"The usefulness learned on the school farm is the very education that is most essential for those who go out as missionaries to many foreign fields."*

Physical Benefits of Agriculture

"Morning exercise, in walking in the free, invigorating air of heaven, or cultivating flowers, small fruits, and vegetables, is necessary to a healthful circulation of the blood. It is the surest safeguard against colds, coughs, congestions of the brain and lungs, inflammation of the liver, the kidneys, and the lungs, and a hundred other diseases" (HR September 1, 1868).

"Those who are old enough should every day that the weather will admit, have a portion of their work in the open air and sunshine. Children and women should not fail to spend some hours each day in exercise out of doors. This has proved a great blessing to me. When in very feeble health, I have occupied some time in my flower garden, and among the small fruits, doing light work, which has never failed to prove a success in recovering my health, and overcoming depression of spirits" (HR April 1, 1871).

"It is for our health and happiness to go out of our houses, and spend as much of our time as possible in the open air. The mind of the invalid should be withdrawn from self, to the beautiful scenes in nature. We can but be cheerful as we listen to the music of the happy birds, and feast our eyes upon flourishing fields and gardens. We should invite our minds to be interested in all the glorious things God has provided for us with a liberal hand. And in reflecting upon these rich tokens of his love and care, we may forget infirmities, be cheerful, and make melody in our hearts unto the Lord" (HR July 1, 1871).

"Those who are feeble and indolent should not yield to inclination to be inactive and deprive themselves of air and sunlight, but should practice exercising out of doors, in walking or working in the garden. They will, without doubt, become very much fatigued; but this will not hurt them. They will experience weariness; yet this will not injure them, but rest will be the sweeter after it. Inaction weakens the organs. And when the muscles that have been idle are used, pain and weariness are experienced because they have become feeble. It is not good policy to give up the use of certain muscles because pain is felt when they are exercised. The pain is frequently caused by the effort of nature to give life and vigor to those parts that have become partially lifeless through inaction. The motion of these long disused muscles will cause pain because nature is awakening them to life" (HR July 1, 1872).

"Those who combine useful physical labor with study have no use for the gymnasium. The benefits of physical labor in the open air have the advantage tenfold to that obtained within doors. The mechanic and the farmer may both labor hard, yet the farmer is the healthier of the two. Nothing short of nature's own sweet air will supply the demands of the system. We should consider that the organs of the body are not a lifeless mass, but the living, active instruments of the soul.

"The old-fashioned farmer, a tiller of the soil, has no need of the gymnasium, for he has all kinds of movements without it. His gymnasium is not confined within walls. His movement room is in the open air. The canopy of heaven is its roof, the solid earth its floor. Here he plows, plants, and hoes. He sows and reaps. In haying, he has a change of movements, he mows and rakes, pitches and tumbles, lifts and loads, throws off and treads down, stows away, and goes through a great variety of movements, which would look nonsensical if his business did not demand all these maneuvers.

"These various motions bring into action the bones, joints, muscles, sinews, and nerves of the body. His exercise makes full, deep, strong inhalations and exhalations necessary, which expand his lungs, purify the blood, sending the warm current of life bounding through arteries and veins. A farmer who is temperate in eating, drinking, and working, usually enjoys health. His tasks are pleasant to him. He has a good appetite. He sleeps well, and may be happy.

"Contrast the active farmer with the student who neglects physical exercise. He bends over his table or desk, his chest is contracted, his lungs crowded. He does not take full, deep inspirations of air. He sits working his brain in a close room, his body as inactive as if he had no particular use for it. His blood moves sluggishly through his system. His feet are cold; his head is hot. How can such have health? It is not the taxation of study that is destroying the health of students; it is the disregard of nature's laws. Physical exercise is essential; this, the farmer gets, but the student does not. Let the taxation come upon the muscles in well-regulated physical labor, which will make the student breathe deep and full, taking into his lungs plenty of the pure, invigorating air of heaven, and he is a new being" (HR September 1, 1873).

[Alternate version] "Those who combine useful labor with study have no need of gymnastic exercises. And work performed in the open air is tenfold more beneficial to health than in-door labor. Both the mechanic and the farmer have physical exercise, yet the farmer is the healthier of the two. Nothing short of nature's invigorating air and sunshine will fully meet the demands of the system. The tiller of the soil finds in his labor all the movements that were ever practiced in the gymnasium. His movement-room is the open fields. The canopy of heaven is its roof, the solid earth its floor. Here he plows and hoes, sows and reaps. Watch him, as in 'haying time' he mows and rakes, pitches and tumbles, lifts and loads, throws off, treads down, and stows away. These various movements call into action the bones, joints, muscles, sinews, and nerves of the body. His vigorous exercise causes full, deep, strong inspirations and exhalations, which expand the lungs and purify the blood, sending the warm current of life bounding through arteries and veins. A farmer who is temperate in all his habits, usually enjoys health. His work is pleasant to him. He has a good appetite. He sleeps well, and may be happy.

"Contrast the condition of the active farmer with that of the student who neglects physical exercise. He sits in a close room, bending over his desk or table, his chest contracted, his lungs crowded. He cannot take full, deep inspirations. His brain is tasked to the utmost, while his body is as inactive as though he had no particular use for it. His blood moves sluggishly through the system. His feet are cold, his head hot. How can such a person have health?" (FE 73, 74, 1923).

"Tell those who are sick that if the hosts of those who are dyspeptics and consumptives could turn farmers they might overcome disease, dispense with drugs and doctors, and recover health" (Lt85-1888).

"The proportionate taxation of the powers of mind and body will prevent the tendency to impure thoughts and actions. Teachers should understand this. They should teach students that pure thoughts and actions are dependent on the way in which they conduct their studies. Conscientious actions are dependent on conscientious thinking. Exercise in agricultural pursuits and in the various branches of labor is a wonderful safeguard against undue brain taxation. No man, woman, or child who fails to use all the powers God has given him can retain his health. He cannot conscientiously keep the commandments of God. He cannot love God supremely and his neighbor as himself" (Lt145-1897).

"Let men and women work in field and orchard and garden. This will bring health and strength to nerve and muscle. Living indoors and cherishing invalidism is a very poor business. If those who are sick will give nerves and muscles and sinews proper exercise in the open air, their health will be renewed.

"The most astonishing ignorance prevails in regard to putting brain, bone, and muscle into active service. Every part of the human organism should be equally taxed. This is necessary for the harmonious development and action of every part" (Lt5-1904).

"So far as possible, all who are seeking to recover health should place themselves amid country surroundings where they can have the benefit of outdoor life. Nature is God's physician. The pure air, the glad sunshine, the flowers and trees, the orchards and vineyards, and outdoor exercise amid these surroundings, are health-giving, life-giving" (MH 263, 1905).

Help for the Poor
"In the country, where fruits and vegetables can be raised in abundance, the poor can be supported at far less expense than in the city where the people must pay cash for nearly everything they live upon.... Almost any of our country churches could easily support two or three worthy families who are unable to support themselves.... In receiving so many of the poor and unfortunate, Battle Creek has robbed other churches of blessings which they might have enjoyed" (RH 1881, date unknown).

"Much might be done in this country [Australia] if there were those who would settle in different localities and cultivate the land as they do in America. Then they would be comparatively independent of the hard times. I think this will be brought about. Most diligent search has been made for a tract of land of several hundred acres on which to locate the school, so that the students may have an opportunity to till the soil, and poor families may have a little piece of land on which to grow vegetables and fruit. This would go far toward sustaining them, and they would have a chance to school their children. But money matters are very close. The people are all hard pressed for means, and know not just what to do unless times change. We must live and have means to carry forward the work" (RH May 29, 1894).

"Thousands of helpless and starving beings, whose numbers are daily swelling the ranks of the criminal classes, might achieve self-support in a happy, healthy, independent life if they could be directed in skillful, diligent labor in the tilling of the soil" (Ed 220, 1903).

Spiritual Lessons From Agriculture

[This is just a sampling of Mrs. White's *many* references to agriculture as it illustrates spiritual/character development]

Abiding in Christ
"You must be full of Christ, and then you will estimate worldly things as God estimates them; and when at work upon your farms or engaged in your business vocations, you will not be separating your souls from God; because you will labor with the true purpose, recognizing God as the owner of all you possess, and will seek wisdom to use his goods in advancing his cause" (Lt70-1886).

"The root of the tree has a double office to fill. It is to hold fast by its tendrils to the earth, while it takes to itself the nourishment desired. Thus it is with the Christian. When his union with Christ, the parent stock, is complete, when he feeds upon him, currents of spiritual strength are given to him. Can the leaves of such a branch wither?—Never! As long as the soul reaches toward Christ, there is little danger that he will wilt, and droop, and decay. The temptations that may come in like a tempest will not uproot him" (YI March 24, 1898).

"Should we go into the garden, and find that there was no sap in the plants, no freshness in the leaves, no bursting buds or blooming flowers, no signs of life in stalk or branches, we would say, 'The plants are dead. Uproot them from the garden; for they are a deformity to the beds.' So it is with those who profess Christianity, and have no spirituality. If there are no signs of religious vigor, if there is no doing of the commandments of the Lord, it is evident that there is no abiding in Christ, the living vine" (YI September 13, 1894).

"The root sends its nourishment through the branch to the outermost twig. So Christ communicates the current of spiritual strength to every believer. So long as the soul is united to Christ, there is no danger that it will wither or decay....

"'And every branch that beareth fruit, he purgeth [pruneth] it, that it may bring forth more fruit.' From the chosen twelve who had followed Jesus, one as a withered branch was about to be taken away; the rest were to pass under the pruning knife of bitter trial. Jesus with solemn tenderness explained the purpose of the husbandman. The pruning will cause pain, but it is the Father who applies the knife. He works with no wanton hand or indifferent heart. There are branches trailing upon the ground; these must be cut loose from the earthly supports to which their tendrils are fastening. They are to reach heavenward, and find their support in God. The excessive foliage that draws away the life current from the fruit must be pruned off. The overgrowth must be cut out, to give room for the healing beams of the Sun of Righteousness. The husbandman prunes away the harmful growth, that the fruit may be richer and more abundant" (DA 676, 1898).

"The object lessons are before us, teaching us valuable lessons, unfolding to us spiritual truth. I have felt sometimes, when my husband was using the knife upon the vines, that he was spoiling them, and I would plead for the vines. I see this thing in an altogether different light now. The Lord has closely connected the spiritual life of man with the plant life, which symbolizes the spiritual experience of all who are seeking to become members of the heavenly family, plants in the Lord's garden. Our lives would be spoiled did not the Lord's pruning knife cut away the objectionable branches, and prune the fruit-bearing branches, that we might bear fruit of a better quality" (Lt6-1900).

"Christ Himself calls our attention to the growth of the vegetable world as an illustration of the agency of His Spirit in sustaining spiritual life. The sap of the vine, ascending from the root, is diffused to the branches, sustaining growth and producing blossoms and fruit. So the life-giving power of the Holy Spirit, proceeding from the Saviour, pervades the soul, renews the motives and affections, and brings even the thoughts into obedience to the will of God, enabling the receiver to bear the precious fruit of holy deeds" (AA 284, 1911).

The Blessings of Manual Labor

"Adam was placed in glorious Eden as the king of the whole earth; yet there was given him a work to do; the Creator required him to dress and take care of the garden. Thus divine wisdom saw it was best for sinless man to have employment; how much more necessary, then, is it for the fallen race to occupy their time with useful labor, thus shutting the door against many temptations, and guarding against the encroachments of the evil one" (HR December 1, 1877).

"Not long since, a young man came to see us about obtaining a situation. Upon inquiry, he said that he had been at work on a farm, but that he could not fix his mind on his work. He desired some other kind of labor, and thought he would give himself to the Lord. Because he did not enjoy the plain, simple duties of life, he concluded to leave them, and devote himself to the cause of God. 'Young man,' said I, 'you are making a mistake. It is necessary that you should prove yourself faithful wherever you are. If called to work upon the farm, or to engage in any of the ordinary duties of life, you should show that you can make a success there; and when you have done this, the Lord may see fit to give you some greater responsibility" (RH March 25, 1880).

"Much more favorable is it for one who has an occupation that keeps him in the open air where his muscles are exercised and his brain equally taxed, and where all the organs are called forth into exercise. Those who live outside the cities, whose labor calls them into the open air, behold the works of the great master Artist in nature, where new scenes are continually unfolding.

"He who makes the book of nature his study...feels a softening subduing influence upon his soul.... The Lord is our Teacher, and if we place ourselves to be instructed by Him, we may learn the most precious lessons from nature" (Ms8-1894).

"There is science in the humblest kind of work, and if all would thus look upon work, they would see its nobility. Heart and soul are to be put into any kind of work that we do; then we do it with cheerfulness and manifest proficiency. Men make manifest the fact that they appreciate God's love in giving them physical and mental powers by the manner in which they do their appointed tasks. Let men employ their educated abilities in devising the best methods of work. Let them remember that there is honor in any class of work that it is essential to do. Where the law of God is made the standard of action, it will ennoble and sanctify all labor. He who is faithful in the discharge of every duty reveals a character that God can approve" (Ms8a-1894).

"The attention of Elijah was attracted to Elisha, the son of Shaphat, who with the servants was plowing with twelve yoke of oxen. He was educator, director, and worker. Elisha did not live in the thickly populated cities. His father was a tiller of the soil, a farmer. Far from city and court dissipation, Elisha had received his education. He had been trained in habits of simplicity, of obedience to his parents and to God. Thus in quietude and contentment he was prepared to do the humble work of cultivating the soil. But though of a meek and quiet spirit, Elisha had no changeable character. Integrity and fidelity and the love and fear of God were his. He had the characteristics of a ruler, but with it all was the meekness of one who would serve. His mind had been exercised in the little things, to be faithful in whatsoever he should do; so that if God should call him to act more directly for him, he would be prepared to hear his voice.

"The surroundings of Elisha's home were those of wealth; but he realized that in order to obtain an all-round education, he must be a constant worker in any work that needed to be done. He had not consented to be in any respect less informed than his father's servants. He had learned how to serve first, that he might know how to lead, instruct, and command.

"Elisha waited contentedly, doing his work with fidelity. Day by day, through practical obedience and the divine grace in which he trusted, he obtained rectitude and strength of purpose. While doing all that he possibly could in co-operating with his father in the home firm, he was doing God's service. He was learning how to co-operate with God" (YI April 14, 1898).

Elisha's father was a wealthy farmer, a man whose household were among the number that in a time of almost universal apostasy had not bowed the knee to Baal. Theirs was a home where God was honored and where allegiance to the faith of ancient Israel was the rule of daily life. In such surroundings the early years of Elisha were passed. In the quietude of country life, under the teaching of God and nature and the discipline of useful work, he received the training in habits of simplicity and of obedience to his parents and to God that helped to fit him for the high position he was afterward to occupy" (PK 217, 1917).

"And Christ has linked His teaching, not only with the day of rest, but with the week of toil. He has wisdom for him who drives the plow and sows the seed. In the plowing and sowing, the tilling and reaping, He teaches us to see an illustration of His work of grace in the heart. So in every line of useful labor and every association of life, He desires us to find a lesson of divine truth. Then our daily toil will no longer absorb our attention and lead us to forget God; it will continually remind us of our Creator and Redeemer. The thought of God will run like a thread of gold through all our homely cares and occupations. For us the glory of His face will again rest upon the face of nature. We shall ever be learning new lessons of heavenly truth, and growing into the image of His purity. Thus shall we 'be taught of the Lord'; and in the lot wherein we are called, we shall 'abide with God.' Isaiah 54:13; 1 Corinthians 7:24" (COL 26, 1900).

"The Lord's purposes are not the purposes of men. He did not design that men should live in idleness. In the beginning He created man a gentleman; but though rich in all that the Owner of the universe could supply, Adam was not to be idle. No sooner was he created than his work was given him. He was to find employment and happiness in tending the things that God had created; and in response to his labor his wants were to be abundantly supplied from the fruits of the garden of Eden.

"While our first parents obeyed God, their labor in the garden was a pleasure; and the earth yielded of its abundance for their wants. But when man departed from obedience, he was doomed to wrestle with the seeds of Satan's sowing, and to earn his bread by the sweat of his brow. Henceforth he must battle in toil and hardship against the power to which he had yielded his will.

"It was God's purpose to alleviate by toil the evil that was brought into the world by man's disobedience. By toil the temptations of Satan might be made ineffectual, and the tide of evil stayed. And though attended with anxiety, weariness, and pain, labor is still a source of happiness and development, and a safeguard against temptation. Its discipline places a check on self-indulgence, and promotes industry, purity, and firmness. Thus it becomes a part of God's great plan for our recovery from the fall" (RH October 3, 1912).

> *"The essential lesson of contented industry in the necessary duties of life is yet to be learned by many of Christ's followers."*

"The essential lesson of contented industry in the necessary duties of life is yet to be learned by many of Christ's followers. It requires more grace, more stern discipline of character, to work for God in the capacity of mechanic, merchant, lawyer, or farmer, carrying the precepts of Christianity into the ordinary business of life, than to labor as an acknowledged missionary in the open field. It requires a strong spiritual nerve to bring religion into the workshop and the business office, sanctifying the details of everyday life, and ordering every transaction according to the standard of God's word. But this is what the Lord requires" (CT 279, 1913).

The Blessings of Trials
"If the Christian thrives and progresses at all, he must do so amid strangers to God, amid scoffing, subject to ridicule. He must stand upright, like the palm-tree in the desert. The sky may be as brass, the desert sand may beat about the palm-tree's roots, and pile itself in heaps about its trunk. Yet the tree lives as an evergreen, fresh and vigorous amid the burning desert sands. Remove the sand till you reach the rootlets of the palm tree, and you discover the secret of its life; it strikes down deep beneath the surface, to the secret waters hidden in the earth. Christians indeed may be fitly represented by the palm tree. They are like Enoch; although surrounded with corrupting influences their faith takes hold of the Unseen. They walk with God, deriving strength and grace from him to withstand the moral pollution surrounding them. Like Daniel in the courts of Babylon, they stand pure and uncontaminated; their life is hid with Christ in God. They are virtuous in spirit amid depravity; they are true and loyal, fervent and zealous, while surrounded by infidels, hypocritical professors, godless and worldly men. Their faith and life are hid with Christ in God. Jesus is in them a well of water springing up into everlasting life. Faith,

like the rootlets of the palm-tree, penetrates beneath the things which are seen, drawing spiritual nourishment from the fountain of life" (RH January 2, 1879).

"A gentleman who was much depressed in spirits by some afflictive providence, was one evening walking in a garden, when he observed a pomegranate tree nearly cut through the stem. Greatly wondering, he asked the gardener the reason, and received an answer that explained to his satisfaction the wounds of his own bleeding heart,—'Sir, this tree used to shoot so strong that it bore nothing but leaves. I was therefore obliged to cut it in this manner, and when it was almost cut through, then it began to bear plenty of fruit'" (RH September 11, 1883).

The Book of Nature
"In the lessons the divine Teacher gave to those who listened to his discourses, he frequently chose a place beautified with flowers, or surrounded with nature's varied scenery, such as, fields, well-cultivated, flourishing gardens, and corn fields, rich verdure, and fruitful trees, green hedges, orange, olive, pomegranate and fig trees, adorning the hills, while in contrast to this flourishing and beautiful scenery, would appear the white rocks and barren soil, while the birds of the air, with their varied music, charmed the ear as they were sporting in the air, or flitting from tree to flower. The majesty of Heaven uses these natural similitudes in representing the word sown in the human heart. He binds up his precious truths with the illustrations of nature that as his hearers shall ever after look upon the objects he has connected with his lessons, the heart will be impressed with the great truths he taught them. He anticipated the fears and anxiety of the listening multitude, and his calm and impressive voice is heard to encourage the flagging faith, and quiet the aroused, distrustful, murmuring fears of his disciples" (HR June 1, 1871).

"The Lord Jesus was the maker of the things in heaven and earth, and the expositor of his own truth, and he called upon nature to reflect the light of the glory of God. The birds of the heaven, the flowers of the field, the trees of the forest, the fruitful fields, the barren land, the grain ripe for the sickle, the fruitless tree, the goings forth of the morning, the setting of the sun, the sowing of the seed, the gathering in of the harvest,—all were employed as emblems of divine truth. He connected the visible works of the Creator with the words of life, and led the mind up from nature to nature's God. Every humble shrub and delicate flower bears testimony to the heart of the love of God. If the eye is not closed, if the ear is not heavy, if the heart is open to receive the impressions of the divine Spirit, nature will speak of the harmony of the natural with the spiritual. Through illustrations drawn from the natural world, Christ has taught lessons of vast importance to the soul; and in thinking of his words while contemplating the object with which he associated his lessons, the divine significance becomes clearer to the mind, and the truth of God enlightens the understanding like a flash of light. Mysteries grow clear, and that which was hard to grasp becomes evident" (ST October 24, 1892).

"The childhood and youth of Christ were spent in humble circumstances, under conditions that were favorable to the development of a sound constitution. His life was passed mostly in the open air. He drank of the pure streams of water, and ate the fruit of the gardens. He passed up and down the steep mountain paths, and through the streets of Nazareth, as he went to and from his place of toil to his home. He enjoyed the varied notes of the birds as they caroled forth their praise to their Creator. He took delight in the beauty of the flowers that decked the fields. He noted with joy the glory of the heavens, the splendor of sun, moon, and stars, and looked upon the rising and setting sun with admiration. The book of nature was open before him, and he enjoyed its tender lessons. The everlasting hills, the olive groves, were favorite places of resort where he went to commune with his Father. He was filled with divine wisdom, and through the study of nature, and by meditation upon and communion with God, his spiritual powers were strengthened.

"In the life of Christ, his childhood and youth, there is a lesson for the youth of today. Christ is our example, and in youth we should contemplate God in nature,—study his character in the work of his hands. The mind is strengthened by becoming acquainted with God, by reading his attributes in the things which he has made. As we behold the beauty and grandeur in the works of nature, our affections go out after God; and though our souls are awed and our spirit subdued, our souls are invigorated by coming in contact with the Infinite through his marvelous works" (YI July 13, 1893).

"The whole natural world is designed to be an interpreter of the things of God. To Adam and Eve in their Eden home, nature was full of the knowledge of God, teeming with divine instruction. It was vocal with the voice of wisdom to their attentive ears. Wisdom spoke to the eye and was received into the heart, for they communed with God in His created works. As soon as the holy pair transgressed the law of the Most High, the brightness from the face of God departed from the face of nature. Nature is now marred and defiled by sin. But God's object lessons are not obliterated; even now, rightly studied and interpreted, she speaks of her Creator....

"The most effective way to teach the heathen who know not God is through His works. In this way, far more readily than by any other method, they can be made to realize the difference between their idols, the works of their own hands, and the true God, the Maker of heaven and earth" (Ms74-1896).

"The book of nature should be studied by all. The soil is cultivated, and the seed is put into the ground. Then God, through his miracle-working power, sends the rain and sunshine, causing the seed to send forth, first the blade, then the ear, and then the corn in the ear. Thus the materials are provided from which man, using his God-given faculties, prepares the loaf which is placed upon the table. In this way God feeds thousands, and ten times ten thousand, a multitude which can not be numbered.

"But men are accustomed to this process, and they drop God out of their thoughts, thinking that they themselves are doing the work. They do not give God the glory due to his name. But it takes just as much power to prepare the harvest which men garner as to make a few barley loaves serve for so many thousands. God gives us all that is needed to sustain life, and in so doing, he is daily working miracles. Were it not for these miracles, which are so graciously repeated in our behalf, we would be weary, hungry, starving, and dying. But God, full of mercy and compassion, constantly cares for us; and because there is no cessation of his goodness, because we are surrounded by his miracles, we cease to appreciate his continually increasing mercies. Fixing our eyes upon human instrumentalities, we give the glory to men, and ascribe the miracles of God to natural causes" (ST August 12, 1897).

"They [the youth] should be taught to till the soil. It would be well if there were, connected with every school, lands for cultivation. Such lands should be regarded as God's own schoolroom. The things of nature should be looked upon as a lesson book which His children are to study, and from which they may obtain knowledge as to the culture of the soul....

"The soil will not produce its riches when worked by impulse. It needs thoughtful, daily attention. It must be plowed often and deep, with a view to keeping out the weeds that take nourishment from the good seed planted. Thus those who plow and sow prepare for the harvest. None need stand in the field amid the sad wreck of their hopes.

"The blessing of the Lord will rest upon those who thus work the land, learning spiritual lessons from nature. In cultivating the soil the worker knows little what treasures will open up before him. While he is not to despise the instruction he may gather from minds that have had an experience, and from the information that intelligent men may impart, he should gather lessons for himself. This is a part of his training. The cultivation of the soil will prove an education to the soul.

"He who causes the seed to spring up, who tends it day and night, who gives it power to develop, is the Author of our being, the King of heaven, and He exercises still greater care and interest in behalf of His children. While the human sower is planting the seed to sustain our earthly life, the Divine Sower will plant in the soul the seed that will bring forth fruit unto life everlasting" (COL 87-89, 1900).

"If the follower of Christ will believe His word and practice it, there is no science in the natural world that he will not be able to grasp and appreciate. There is nothing but that will furnish him means for imparting the truth to others. Natural science is a treasure house of knowledge from which every student in the school of Christ may draw. As we contemplate the beauty of nature, as we study its lessons in the cultivation of the soil, in the growth of the trees, in all the wonders of earth and sea and sky, there will come to us a new perception of truth. And the mysteries connected with God's dealings with men, the depths of His wisdom and judgment as seen in human life—these are found to be a storehouse rich in treasure" (COL 125, 1900).

"In his teaching, Christ called the attention of his hearers to the things of nature, the work of his own hands. He made the trees, the grass, the flowers, that they might teach us precious lessons. Nature was to him a great lesson-book, by which he sought to open the eyes of human beings to the love and power of God.

"Nature is a lesson-book to which all, high and low, rich and poor, may have access; and from it the most helpful lessons may be learned. Ever in its varying seasons it repeats its lessons, that by its representations, man may grasp heavenly truth. The apparently commonplace things of earth are silent teachers, instructing us in purity, industry, economy, and patience" (YI August 16, 1900).

"The God of nature is perpetually at work. His infinite power works unseen, but manifestations appear in the effects which the work produces. The same God who guides the planets works in the fruit orchard and in the vegetable garden. He never made a thorn, a thistle, or a tare. These are Satan's work, the result of degeneration, introduced by him among the precious things; but it is through God's immediate agency that every bud bursts into blossom. When He was in the world in the form of humanity, Christ said: 'My Father worketh hitherto, and I work.' John 5:17. So when the students employ their time and strength in agricultural work, in heaven it is said of them, Ye 'are labourers together with God' 1 Corinthians 3:9" (6T 186, 1901).

"As we look at a beautiful garden, with its opening buds, let us remember that this is an expression of our Father's love. As we note the varied tints of the flowers and inhale their delicate fragrance, let us think of the words, 'Consider the lilies of the field, how they grow; they toil not, neither do they spin: and yet I say unto you, That even Solomon in all his glory was not arrayed like one of these.' God has given us the flowers to teach us lessons of trust. 'Wherefore, if God so clothe the grass of the field, which today is, and tomorrow is cast into the oven, shall he not much more clothe you, O ye of little faith?' If the great Master Artist makes perfect and lovely that which is today, and tomorrow is cast into the oven, will he not care much more for the beings purchased by the blood of his only begotten Son?

"We are pilgrims and strangers on this earth, looking for a city which hath foundations, whose builder and maker is God. The path in which we travel is narrow, and calls for self-denial and self-sacrifice. We meet with trial and conflict. But God has not left us to travel without help. Our pathway to the heavenly Canaan is bordered with the fair flowers of promise. They blossom all along the way, sending forth their rich fragrance, like the flowers in the gardens of this earth" (YI January 23, 1902).

"Thus while the children and youth gain a knowledge of facts from teachers and textbooks, let them learn to draw lessons and discern truth for themselves. In their gardening, question them as to what they learn from the care of their plants. As they look on a beautiful landscape, ask them why God clothed the fields and woods with such lovely and varied hues. Why was not all colored a somber brown? When they gather the flowers, lead them to think why He spared us the beauty of these wanderers from Eden. Teach them to notice the evidences everywhere manifest in nature of God's thought for us, the wonderful adaptation of all things to our need and happiness.

"He alone who recognizes in nature his Father's handiwork, who in the richness and beauty of the earth reads the Father's handwriting—he alone learns from the things of nature their deepest lessons, and receives their highest ministry. Only he can fully appreciate the significance of hill and vale, river and sea, who looks upon them as an expression of the thought of God, a revelation of the Creator.

"Many illustrations from nature are used by the Bible writers, and as we observe the things of the natural world, we shall be enabled, under the guiding of the Holy Spirit, more fully to understand the lessons of God's word. It is thus that nature becomes a key to the treasure house of the word" (Ed 119, 120, 1903).

"The Redeemer has warned us against the pride of life, but not against its grace and natural beauty. He pointed to the glowing beauty of the flowers of the field, and said, 'Consider the lilies of the field, how they grow; they toil not, neither do they spin; and yet I say unto you, That even Solomon in all his glory was not arrayed like one of these.' Here He shows that, even though persons may toil with weariness to make themselves objects of admiration, that which they value so highly will not bear comparison with the flowers of the field. Even these simple flowers, with God's adornment, would outvie in loveliness the gorgeous apparel of Solomon. In the growth and development of nature, learn the principles of Christ's kingdom. Thus the light of heaven will quicken the mind. Christ Himself will be your teacher. Those who combine with their school education a knowledge of God's working through physical life, in the garden of nature, will receive lessons simple, yet full of instruction, in regard to His working through spiritual life, in the garden of the heart" (ST December 6, 1905).

Cooperation with God
"God's blessings are not bestowed upon men independent of human effort. We see this principle illustrated in the natural world. God has given us the earth with its treasures. He causes it to bring forth food for man and beast, he sends the recurring seasons, he gives the sunshine, the dew, and the rain; yet man is required to act his part; he must co-operate with God's plan by diligent, painstaking effort. The plough must break up the soil, the seed must be sown, the field must be tilled, or there will be no harvest.

"So in the spiritual world. All that we possess, whether of talents, of influence, or of means, is of God; we can accomplish nothing without divine aid. Yet we are not released from the necessity of effort. While salvation is the gift of God, man has a part to act in the carrying out of the plan of redemption. God has chosen to use men as his instruments, to employ human agencies in the accomplishment of his purposes. He has ordained to unite divine power with human endeavor, in the work of saving souls. Thus we become laborers together with God. We have a grand and important work, because it is a part of God's great plan for the redemption of man. It is a high honor bestowed upon finite beings thus to co-operate with the Majesty of heaven" (RH December 7, 1886).

"Those who teach in Sabbath school must have their hearts warmed and invigorated by the truth of God, being not hearers only, but also doers of the word. They should be nourished in Christ as the branches are nourished in the vine. The dews of heavenly grace should fall upon them, that their hearts may be like precious plants, whose buds open and expand and give forth a grateful fragrance as flowers in the garden of God. Teachers should be diligent students of the word of God, and ever reveal the fact that they are learning daily lessons in the school of Christ, and are able to communicate to others the light they have received from Him who is the great Teacher, the Light of the world" (SSW April 1, 1892).

"The Lord alone can give the precious former and latter rain. The clouds, the sunshine, the dews at night—these are heaven's most precious provisions. But all these favors graciously bestowed of Heaven will prove of little worth to those who do not appropriate them by diligent, painstaking effort on their part. Personal efforts must be put forth in agriculture. There is the plowing and replowing. Implements must be brought in and human skill must use them. The seed must be sown in its season. The laws which control seed time and harvest must be observed, else there will be no harvest" (Ms182-1897).

"The man who sows apparently throws away the seed upon which he and his family depend for a livelihood. But he is only giving up a present advantage for a much larger return. He throws the seed away that he may gather it again in an abundant harvest. His dependent family may look forward in faith to large returns.

"From the work of seed-sowing most precious lessons may be taught in the family. The children may be instructed to grasp by faith unseen benefits.

The influence of God's miracle-working power is to be shown in the lessons given from nature in our families and in our school. The combined influence of the Lord's unseen agencies are necessary to the harvesting of the precious crops that come from the seed buried in the ground. The fields must have care; and when the sower has done his work of casting the seed into the ground, this is only the beginning of the end. A watchful caretaker is needed over the seed. When man has done his part in preparing the soil, enriching it if needs be, and planting the seed, showing care, thoughtfulness, and understanding in the work, he must depend upon God, the great Husbandman to send sunshine and showers, to give heat and moisture to the thirsty fields.

"If these thoughts could be awakened in children's minds, if they could be led to understand the wonderful work of God in supplying His large family in our world with the necessities of life, they would realize more of His power. He employs many unseen agencies to make the seeds, apparently thrown away, living plants. First appears the blade, then the ear, then the full corn in the ear. God created the electricity that gives life to the seed, vitality to the blade, the ear, and the corn in the ear. Who else can be depended on to give the due proportion required of all the agencies to perfect the harvest of fruits and grains? Let man employ his agencies to the utmost limit; he must then depend on his Creator, who knows just what is needed for the harvest, which is connected to Him by wonderful links of His own wonderful power, beyond the human agency. Without these unseen agencies, seed is valueless.

"Christ taught His disciples to pray, 'Give us this day our daily bread.' The Lord hears this prayer, and is constantly working to answer it. He lets His sun shine upon the just and the unjust, and gives to all refreshing showers, wind, and rain, thunder and lightning. All are God's blessing, sent to purify the atmosphere from injurious unhealthful agencies, which if allowed to accumulate, would poison the atmosphere and destroy everything that breathes the breath of life" (Ms34-1898).

"They [our brethren] are to understand that the garden of the heart is to be cultivated, the weeds diligently uprooted.

"As they cultivate the soil, the students are to learn spiritual lessons. The plough must break up the fallow ground. It must lie under the rays of the sun and the purifying air. Then the seed, to all appearance dead, is to be dropped into the prepared soil. Trees are to be planted, seeds for vegetables sown. And after man has acted his part, God's miracle-working power gives life and vitality to the things placed in the soil. In this agricultural process, there are lessons to be learned. Man is not to do slothful work. He is to act the part appointed him by God. His industry is essential if he would have a harvest. And just such a work is to be done in the human mind and heart" (Ms71-1898).

[Alternate version] "As we cultivate the soil day by day, we may learn precious spiritual lessons. The fallow ground of the heart must be broken up. It must be warmed by the rays of the sun, and purified by the air. Then the seed, to all appearance lifeless and inactive, is to be dropped into the soil prepared for its reception. Trees also are to be planted, and cultivated with care. And after man has done his part, God's miracle-working power gives life and vitality to the things placed in the soil. Man is not to overlook the power of God, nor is he to neglect his part of the work, appointed to him by God. Man is not to be slothful. His industry is essential if he would have a harvest. And so it is with the work to be done in the human heart and mind. 'The seed is the word of God.' 'He that soweth the good seed is the Son of man'" (RH October 18, 1898).

"Those who till the soil have the illustration ever before them. Year by year man preserves his supply of grain by apparently throwing away the choicest part. For a time it must be hidden under the furrow, to be watched over by the Lord. Then appears the blade, then the ear, and then the corn in the ear. But this development cannot take place unless the grain is buried out of sight, hidden, and to all appearance, lost" (DA 623, 1898).

"Next to the Bible, nature is to be our great lesson book. But there is no virtue in deifying nature, for this is exalting the thing made above the great Master Artist who designed the work, and who keeps it every hour operating according to His appointment. As we plant the seed, and cultivate the plant, we are to remember that God created the seed, and He gives it to the earth. By His divine power He cares for that seed. It is by His appointment that the seed in dying gives its life to the blade, which contains in itself other seeds to be treasured and again put into the earth to yield their harvest. We may also study how the co-operation of man acts a part. The human agent has his part to act, his work to do. This is one of the lessons which nature teaches, and we shall see in it a solemn, a beautiful work" (AUCR July 31, 1899).

"Special laws were given to the Israelites in regard to the tilling of the soil. 'And the Lord spake unto Moses in mount Sinai, saying, Speak unto the children of Israel, and say unto them, When ye come into the land which I give you, then shall the land keep a sabbath unto the Lord. Six years thou shalt sow thy field, and six years thou shalt prune thy vineyard, and gather in the fruit thereof; But in the seventh year shall be a sabbath of rest unto the land, a sabbath for the Lord: thou shalt neither sow thy field, nor prune thy vineyard. That which groweth of its own accord of thy harvest thou shalt not reap, neither gather the grapes of thy vine undressed: for it is a year of rest unto the land. And the sabbath of the land shall be meat for you; for thee, and for thy servant, and for thy maid, and for thy hired servant, and for thy stranger that sojourneth with thee. And for thy cattle, and for the beast that are in thy land, shall all the increase thereof be meat. Lev. 25:1-7.

"These laws seem peculiar to those who have not known God's statutes; but the Lord knew better than man what arrangements to make with His people. These laws were written down, and the seventh year after they [Israel] settled in Canaan was to be a Sabbath year. All agricultural business was to stop. There was to be no planting or sowing. For one year the people were to depend wholly on the Lord, having faith in His arrangements as the Householder. The land needed a rest in order to renew the forces necessary for growth. That which grew of itself was the common property of the poor and the stranger, the cattle and the herds. Thus the land was to receive rest, and the poor and the cattle a feast.

"This was to show that nature was not God, that God controlled nature. God designed that from nature His church should constantly learn important lessons. They were to cherish a vivid sense that God was the Manager, the Householder. They were to know the reality of His presence and His providential care over all the earth. They were to realize that all nature was under His supervision, all the productions of the ground under His ministration. This was to give them faith in His providence. He could withhold His blessings or bestow them....

"If the people chose to manage the land in their own supposed wisdom, they would find that the Lord would not work a miracle to counteract the evils He was trying to save them from.

"The Lord presented to His people the course they must pursue if they would be a prosperous, independent nation. If they obeyed Him, He declared that health and peace would be theirs, and under His supervision the land would yield its increase. The tithing system was instituted by the Lord as the very best arrangement to help the people in carrying out the principles of the law. If this law were obeyed, the people would be entrusted with the entire vineyard, the whole earth.

"'Wherefore ye shall do my statutes, and keep my judgments, and do them; and ye shall dwell in the land in safety. And the land shall yield her fruit, and ye shall eat your fill, and dwell therein in safety. And if ye shall say, What shall we eat the seventh year? behold, we shall not sow, nor gather in our increase: Then I will command my blessing upon you in the sixth year, and it shall bring forth fruit for three years. And ye shall sow the eighth year, and eat yet of old fruit until the ninth year; until her fruits come in ye shall eat of the old store. Lev. 25:18-22.

"The children of Israel were given laws and regulations which would give all nations on the earth a true idea of God's kingdom and government. As a nation, as families, as individuals, they were to obey these laws. They were to be a kingdom of priests and princes. Those who felt their entire dependence on God, looking to Him for instruction and relying upon Him for power to carry out His plans in the vineyard they were to cultivate, would receive the largest blessing and revenue.

"Adam and Eve lost Eden, and because of their sin the land was cursed; yet if God's people obeyed His requirements and followed His directions in regard to tilling the soil, the land would be brought back to a prosperous and beautiful condition. Men were to cooperate with God in restoring the diseased land to health, that it might be a praise and a glory to His name. And as the land they possessed would if managed with skill and earnestness, produce its treasures, so their hearts, if controlled by God, would reflect His character.

"But if because of selfishness and covetousness men felt capable of managing without the wisdom of God, if they looked upon the land as their own, and refused to give it a sabbath, it would lose its vigor, and dearth and sickness would testify to their disobedience.

"In the laws which God gave for the cultivation of the soil, He was giving the people opportunity to overcome their selfishness and become heavenly-minded. Canaan would be to them as Eden if they obeyed the word of the Lord. Through them the Lord designed to teach all the nations of the world how to cultivate the soil so that it would yield healthy fruit, free from disease. The earth is the Lord's vineyard, and is to be treated according to His plan. Those who cultivated the soil were to realize that they were doing God service. They were as truly in their lot and place as

> *"Those who cultivated the soil were to realize that they were doing God service. They were as truly in their lot and place as were the men appointed to minister in the priesthood."*

were the men appointed to minister in the priesthood and in work connected with the tabernacle. God told the people that the Levites were a gift to them, and no matter what their trade, they were to help to support them. Especially were those tilling the soil to bring in the rich treasures of the earth for the sustenance of the Levites" (Ms121-1899).

"In order for the seed to grow, it must have care; and when man has done his part, this is only the beginning. After man has prepared the soil, and planted the seed, showing care and thoughtfulness in the work, he must depend upon God, the great Husbandman, to send sunshine and showers to water the thirsty ground, and cause the seed to spring up and grow. The combined influence of the Lord's unseen agencies is necessary from the time the seed is buried in the ground till the harvest is gathered.

"If we understood better the wonderful work of God in supplying his family on the earth with the necessities of life, we should know more of his power. He employs many unseen agencies to make the seed spring up and grow. It is his power that gives life to the seed. Without his power how could the harvest be perfected? Let man do his utmost, and he must still depend on the Creator, who understands just what is needed for the perfection of the fruit.

"Christ taught his disciples to pray, 'Give us this day our daily bread.' God hears this prayer, and is constantly working to answer it. He makes his sun to shine on the just and on the unjust, and gives to all wind and rain, thunder and lightning. These are God's blessings, sent to purify the atmosphere from injurious, unhealthful agencies, which, if allowed to accumulate, would poison it, and destroy everything that breathes the breath of life" (YI August 16, 1900).

"Of the almost innumerable lessons taught in the varied processes of growth, some of the most precious are conveyed in the Saviour's parable of the growing seed. It has lessons for old and young.

"'So is the kingdom of God, as if a man should cast seed into the ground; and should sleep, and rise night and day, and the seed should spring and grow up, he knoweth not how. For the earth bringeth forth fruit of herself; first the blade, then the ear, after that the full corn in the ear.' Mark 4:26-28.

"The seed has in itself a germinating principle, a principle that God Himself has implanted; yet if left to itself the seed would have no power to spring up. Man has his part to act in promoting the growth of the grain; but there is a point beyond which he can accomplish nothing. He must depend upon One who has connected the sowing and the reaping by wonderful links of His own omnipotent power.

"There is life in the seed, there is power in the soil; but unless infinite power is exercised day and night, the seed will yield no return. The showers of rain must refresh the thirsty fields; the sun must impart warmth; electricity must be conveyed to the buried seed. The life which the Creator has implanted, He alone can call forth. Every seed grows, every plant develops, by the power of God.

"'The seed is the word of God.' 'As the earth bringeth forth her bud, and as the garden causeth the things that are sown in it to spring forth; so the Lord God will cause righteousness and praise to spring forth.' Luke 8:11; Isaiah 61:11. As in the natural, so in the spiritual sowing; the power that alone can produce life is from God" (Ed 104, 1903).

"The plant grows by receiving that which God has provided to sustain its life. So spiritual growth is attained through co-operation with divine agencies. As the plant takes root in the soil, so we are to take root in Christ. As the plant receives the sunshine, the dew, and the rain, so are we to receive the Holy Spirit. If our hearts are stayed upon Christ, He will come unto us 'as the rain, as the latter and former rain unto the earth.' As the Sun of Righteousness, He will arise upon us 'with healing in his wings.' We shall 'grow as the lily.' We 'shall revive as the corn, and grow as the vine.' Hosea 6:3; Malachi 4:2; Hosea 14:5, 7" (Ed 106, 1903).

"In the Saviour's miracle of feeding the five thousand is illustrated the working of God's power in the production of the harvest. Jesus draws aside the veil from the world of nature and reveals the creative energy that is constantly exercised for our good. In multiplying the seed cast into the ground, He who multiplied the loaves is working a miracle every day. It is by miracle that He constantly feeds millions from earth's harvest fields. Men are called upon to co-operate with Him in the care of the grain and the preparation of the loaf, and because of this they lose sight of the divine agency. The working of His power is ascribed to natural causes or to human instrumentality, and too often His gifts are perverted to selfish uses and made a curse instead of a blessing. God is seeking to change all this. He desires that our dull senses shall be quickened to discern His merciful kindness, that His gifts may be to us the blessing that He intended.

"It is the word of God, the impartation of His life, that gives life to the seed; and of that life, we, in eating the grain, become partakers. This, God desires us to discern; He desires that even in receiving our daily bread we may recognize His agency and may be brought into closer fellowship with Him.

"By the laws of God in nature, effect follows cause with unvarying certainty. The reaping testifies to the sowing. Here no pretense is tolerated. Men may deceive their fellow men and may receive praise and compensation for service which they have not rendered. But in nature there can be no deception. On the unfaithful husbandman the harvest passes sentence of condemnation. And in the highest sense this is true also in the spiritual realm. It is in appearance, not in reality, that evil succeeds. The child who plays truant from school, the youth who is slothful in his studies, the clerk or apprentice who fails of serving the interests of his employer, the man in any business or profession who is untrue to his highest responsibilities, may flatter himself that, so long as the wrong is concealed, he is gaining an advantage. But not so; he is cheating himself. The harvest of life is character, and it is this that determines destiny, both for this life and for the life to come" (Ed 107, 108, 1903).

"We may learn a precious lesson from the work of the farmer in cultivating his field. In order to reap a harvest, he must co-operate with God, the great Husbandman. His part is to prepare the ground and plant the seed, at the right time and in the right way. God gives the seed life. He sends the sunshine and the showers, and the seed springs up, 'first the blade, then the ear, after that the full corn in the ear.' If the farmer fails to do his part, the sun may shine, the dew and the showers may fall upon the soil, but there will be no harvest. And though the work of planting had been done, unless God sent the sunshine and the dew and the rain, the seed would never, never spring up and grow.

"So, in the cultivation of the Christian graces, we must co-operate with God. His Word tells us to work out our own salvation; and it adds, 'For it is God which worketh in you both to will and to do of his good pleasure.' We have a part to act, and, as we act this part, God will surely co-operate with us" (PUR January 5, 1905).

"God has given man land to be cultivated. But in order that the harvest may be reaped, there must be harmonious action between divine and human agencies. The plow and other implements of labor must be used at the right time. The seed must be sown in its season. Man is not to fail of doing his part. If he is careless and negligent, his unfaithfulness testifies against him. The harvest is proportionate to the energy he has expended.

"So it is in spiritual things. We are to be laborers together with God. Man is to work out his own salvation with fear and trembling, for it is God that worketh in him, both to will and to do of his good pleasure. There is to be co-partnership, a divine relation, between the Son of God and the repentant sinner. We are made sons and daughters of God. 'As many as received him, to them gave he power to become the sons of God.' Christ provides the mercy and grace so abundantly given to all who believe in him. He fulfils the terms upon which salvation rests. But we must act our part by accepting the blessing in faith. God works and man works. Resistance of temptation must come from man, who must draw his power from God. Thus he becomes a co-partner with Christ" (RH May 28, 1908).

"For over a year the temple was neglected and well-nigh forsaken. The people dwelt in their homes and strove to attain temporal prosperity, but their situation was deplorable. Work as they might they did not prosper. The very elements of nature seemed to conspire against them. Because they had let the temple lie waste, the Lord sent upon their substance a wasting drought. God had bestowed upon them the fruits of field and garden, the corn and the wine and the oil, as a token of His favor; but because they had used these bountiful gifts so selfishly, the blessings were removed" (PK 573, 1917).

The Garden of the Lord
"A grove of evergreens was presented before me. Several, including myself, were laboring among them. I was bidden to closely inspect the trees and see if they were in a flourishing condition. I observed that some were being bent and deformed by the wind, and needed to be supported by stakes. I was carefully removing the dirt from the feeble and dying trees to ascertain the cause of their condition. I discovered worms at the roots of some. Others had not been watered properly and were dying from drought. The roots of others had been crowded together to their injury. My work was to explain to the workmen the different reasons why these trees did not prosper. This was necessary from the fact that trees in other grounds were liable to be affected as these had been, and the cause of their not flourishing and how they should be cultivated and treated must be made known" (1T 632, 1868).

"Your first ministerial field is to guard and train your children, taking care of the little garden God has given you; and when you educate and train these children, then you have done a work that God will bless" (Ms13-1886).

"'Ye are God's husbandry.' As one takes pleasure in the cultivation of a garden, so God takes pleasure in his believing sons and daughters. A garden demands constant labor. The weeds must be removed; new plants must be set out; branches that are making too rapid development must be pruned back. So the Lord works for his garden, so he tends his plants. He cannot take pleasure in any development that does not reveal the graces of the character of Christ. The blood of Christ has made men and women God's precious charge. Then how careful should we be not to manifest too much freedom in pulling up the plants that God has placed in his garden! Some plants are so feeble that they have hardly any life, and for these the Lord has a special care" (RH August 24, 1897).

> *"The law is the root, the gospel is the fragrant blossom and fruit which it bears."*

"No man can rightly present the law of God without the gospel, or the gospel without the law. The law is the gospel embodied, and the gospel is the law unfolded. The law is the root, the gospel is the fragrant blossom and fruit which it bears" (COL 128, 1900).

"The husbandman chooses a piece of land from the wilderness; he fences, clears, and tills it, and plants it with choice vines, expecting a rich harvest. This plot of ground, in its superiority to the uncultivated waste, he expects to do him honor by showing the results of his care and toil in its cultivation. So God had chosen a people from the world to be trained and educated by Christ. The prophet says, 'The vineyard of the Lord of hosts is the house of Israel, and the men of Judah His pleasant plant.' Isaiah 5:7. Upon this people God had bestowed great privileges, blessing them richly from His abundant goodness. He looked for them to honor Him by yielding fruit. They were to reveal the principles of His kingdom. In the midst of a fallen, wicked world they were to represent the character of God.

"As the Lord's vineyard they were to produce fruit altogether different from that of the heathen nations. These idolatrous peoples had given themselves up to work wickedness. Violence and crime, greed, oppression, and the most corrupt practices, were indulged without restraint. Iniquity, degradation, and misery were the fruits of the corrupt tree. In marked contrast was to be the fruit borne on the vine of God's planting.

"It was the privilege of the Jewish nation to represent the character of God as it had been revealed to Moses. In answer to the prayer of Moses, 'Show me Thy glory,' the Lord promised, 'I will make all My goodness pass before thee.' Exodus 33:18, 19. 'And the Lord passed by before him, and proclaimed, The Lord, the Lord God, merciful and gracious, longsuffering, and abundant in goodness and truth, keeping mercy for thousands, forgiving iniquity and transgression and sin.' Exodus 34:6, 7. This was the fruit that God desired from His people. In the purity of their characters, in the holiness of their lives, in their mercy and loving-kindness and compassion, they were to show that 'the law of the Lord is perfect, converting the soul.' Psalm 19:7" (COL 285, 1900).

"From the endless variety of plants and flowers, we may learn an important lesson. All blossoms are not the same in form or color. Some possess healing virtues. Some are always fragrant. There are professing Christians who think it their duty to make every other Christian like themselves. This is man's plan, not the plan of God. In the church of God there is room for characters as varied as are the flowers in a garden. In His spiritual garden there are many varieties of flowers" (Lt95-1902).

"From San Diego we returned to Los Angeles, and on Tuesday, December 6, we went to Redlands for a few days' visit. A little way out from Los Angeles, the scenery became very uninteresting. We passed through much barren land. Here and there, the desert, by means of irrigation, had been converted into flourishing orange groves; but for miles and miles at a stretch the land was uncultivated. As we rode along, I remembered scenes presented to me years before, of barren land, such as that through which we were passing, being cultivated and improved, and, by irrigation, made to yield rich returns. I was instructed that this was an object-lesson of the influence that the saving grace of Christ should have upon the hearts and lives of human beings. And had those to whom God has given the riches of the water of life, realized the responsibilities resting upon them as stewards of the grace of God, and gone forth as faithful missionaries into all the barren places of the earth, the wilderness would have been made to blossom as the garden of the Lord" (RH March 30, 1905).

"Gather the Roses"

"If Christians would manifest the joy that Christ is willing to give them, they would represent the religion of the Bible much better than they now do. We are to be in the world, but we are not to be of it. We are to see and appreciate all the beauties in nature, and we are to let the favors of God lift up our minds to the bountiful Giver. We are to express, by precept and example, that we are the possessors of peace, and trust, and fullness of joy. We are to cultivate gratitude and love and praise in our hearts, that through his promises, richer than precious pearls, we may discern the purposes of God toward us. As the flowers gather for themselves the hidden properties of earth and air, and develop into things of beauty to delight our senses, so Christians are privileged to gather from the garden of God's promises, faith and hope, peace, joy, and support. They are to give out again to others a life fragrant with good works" (ST June 29, 1888).

"When I was in Europe, a sister wrote to me in the deepest distress. She was in despair, and she wrote, 'Can't you say a word of encouragement to me? Can't you tell me of anything I could do to be relieved of my burden?' The night after I had read her letter, I dreamed that I was in a garden, and a stately personage was conducting me through its paths. I was picking the flowers and enjoying the fragrance, when this sister, who was walking by my side, called my attention to some unsightly thistles that were impeding her way. There she was, mourning and grieving. She was not walking in the pathway, following the guide, but was walking among the briers and thorns. 'Oh,' she mourned, 'is it not a pity that this beautiful garden is spoiled with thorns?' Then the guide turned, and said, 'Let the thistles alone, for they will only wound you. Gather the roses, and the lilies, and the pinks;' and now she is doing this. Why not have something pleasant to think about? 'Whatsoever things are true, whatsoever things are honest, whatsoever things are just, whatsoever things are pure, whatsoever things are lovely, whatsoever things are of good report; if there be any virtue, and if there be any praise, think on these things.'

"Suppose you had a family of children to whom you gave many pleasant and useful things, and they should pick out something that did not seem without objection to them, and should talk of its defects, and mourn and fret because this one thing did not quite meet their approval; how would you think they were repaying your goodness and kindness to them? Would you feel that your efforts were rewarded as they should be? Would it not grieve your heart to find your children so ungrateful, and so unappreciative of your love toward them?

"The precious Bible is the garden of God, and his promises are the lilies, and the roses, and the pinks. Why do you not gather the fragrant flowers, and leave the thistles alone? Why do you not dwell on the love of Jesus? Why do you not bring gratitude into your life for all the benefits you have received from your Heavenly Father? The more thankfulness you express, the more you will have to express" (RH March 19, 1889).

"Suppose you were in a garden where bloomed beautiful roses, and lilies, and pinks; but instead of gathering the beautiful flowers, you should seek for everything objectionable to take away to show to others as a sample of that garden. Would the objectionable things you had gathered properly represent the garden?—By no means. If Christians gather up gloom and sadness to their souls, and murmur and complain, are they representing God and the Christian life as it really is? Christ tells us that if we abide in him, he will abide in us. Are we doing as he has bidden us? Will we gather the roses and the lilies and the pinks, and present to the world the hopeful, bright side of religion?" (RH April 16, 1889).

The Little Things

"If parents desire to teach their children self-control, they must first form the habit themselves. The scolding and fault-finding of parents, encourages a hasty, passionate temper in their children. Love and justice should stand side by side in the government of the household. Let prompt obedience to parental authority be invariably enforced. God has given parents their work, to form the characters of their children after the Divine Pattern. By his grace, they can accomplish the task; but it will require patient, painstaking effort, no less than firmness and decision, to guide the will and restrain the passions. A field left to itself produces only thorns and briers. He who would secure a harvest for usefulness or beauty must first prepare the soil and sow the seed, then dig about the young shoots, removing the weeds and softening the earth, and the precious plants will flourish and richly repay his care and labor" (ST November 24, 1881).

"Your afflicted son needs to be dealt with calmly and tenderly; he needs your compassion. He should not be exposed to your insane temper and unreasonable demands. You must reform in respect to the spirit you manifest. Ungovernable passion will not be subdued in a moment; but your lifework is before you to rid the garden of the heart of the poisonous weeds of impatience, faultfinding, and an overbearing disposition. 'The fruit of the Spirit is love, joy, peace, longsuffering, gentleness, goodness, faith, meekness, temperance.' They that are Christ's have crucified the flesh, with its affections and lusts; but the brutish part of your nature takes the lines of control and guides the spiritual. This is God's order reversed" (4T 365, 1881).

> *"Parents, your own home is the first field in which you are called to labor. The precious plants in the home garden demand your first care.*

"Parents, your own home is the first field in which you are called to labor. The precious plants in the home garden demand your first care. To you it is appointed to watch for souls as they that must give an account. Carefully consider your work, its nature, its bearing, and its results. Line upon line, precept upon precept, here a little and there a little, you must instruct, warn, and counsel, ever remembering that your looks, words, and actions have a direct bearing upon the future course of your dear ones. Your work is not to paint a form of beauty upon canvas, or to chisel it from marble; but to impress upon a human soul the image of the Divine" (ST May 25, 1882).

"The teacher should carefully study the disposition and character of his pupils, that he may adapt his teaching to their peculiar needs. He has a garden to tend, in which are plants differing widely in nature, form, and development. While a few may appear beautiful and symmetrical, many others have become dwarfed and misshapen by neglect. The preceding gardener has not done his work faithfully. By proper cultivation these plants and shrubs might have been made to grow up comely and beautiful; but those to whom was committed the care of the tender plantlets, left them to the mercy of circumstances, and now the work of training and cultivation is increased tenfold" (RH September 22, 1885).

"In this world we have temporal duties to perform, and in the performance of these duties we are forming characters that will either stand the test of the judgment or be weighed in the balances and found wanting. We may do the smallest duties nobly, firmly, faithfully, as if seeing the whole heavenly host looking upon us. Take a lesson from the gardener. If he wishes a plant to grow, he cultivates and trims it; he gives water, he digs about its roots, plants it where the sunshine will fall upon it, and day by day he works about it; and not by violent efforts, but by acts constantly repeated, he trains the shrub until its form is perfect, and its bloom is full. The grace of our Lord Jesus Christ works upon the heart and mind as an educator. The continued influence of his Spirit upon the soul, trains and molds and fashions the character after the divine model. Let the youth bear in mind that a repetition of acts, forms habit, and habit, character. 'Watch ye therefore, and pray always, that ye may be accounted worthy to escape all these things that shall come to pass, and to stand before the Son of man.' Are you, my youthful friends, able to look forward with joyful hope and expectancy toward the day when the Lord, the righteous Judge, shall appear? and will he confess your name before the Father and before his holy angels?" (YI September 7, 1893).

"If you would skilfully [sic] cultivate and train your flowers, you must consult a gardener; for he understands the work, he trains them to grow how and where he will. He gives them plenty of water, sunshine, and air, and digs about their roots. Day by day he works, not by violent efforts, but by little acts constantly repeated, until he can train shrub and flower into perfect form and beauty. Thus the grace of Christ works upon the human mind and heart as an educator. The continued influence of his Spirit trains the soul, molding the character after the divine Model" (YI January 28, 1897).

"Parents, in the training of your children, study the lessons that God has given in nature. If you would train a pink, or rose, or lily, how would you do it? Ask the gardener by what process he makes every branch and leaf to flourish so beautifully, and to develop in symmetry and loveliness. He will tell you that it was by no rude touch, no violent effort; for this would only break the delicate stems. It was by little attentions, often repeated. He moistened the soil, and protected the growing plants from the fierce blasts and from the scorching sun, and God caused them to flourish and to blossom into loveliness. In dealing with your children, follow the method of the gardener. By gentle touches, by loving ministrations, seek to fashion their characters after the pattern of the character of Christ" (DA 516, 1898).

"Children are not to be left to grow as they will. As the gardener straightens the young trees in an orchard, so they are to be straightened. Their perversity is to be checked; for if this is not done, they will carry it with them into the religious life, and it will make them crooked church members. Parents who think there is no need of restraining their children, who allow them to shape their own character, will see in the future the sad result of this neglect. They will see that their failure to point out and correct defects has made it impossible for their children to enter heaven" (ST December 11, 1901).

"Parents and teachers should seek most earnestly for that wisdom which Jesus is ever ready to give; for they are dealing with human minds at the most interesting and impressible period of their development. They should aim so to cultivate the tendencies of the youth that at each stage of their life they may represent the natural beauty appropriate to that period, unfolding gradually, as do the plants and flowers in the garden" (6T 204, 1901).

"The son of a wealthy farmer, Elisha had taken up the work that lay nearest. While possessing the capabilities of a leader among men, he received a training in life's common duties. In order to direct wisely, he must learn to obey. By faithfulness in little things, he was prepared for weightier trusts" (Ed 58, 1903).

"Because they are not connected with some directly religious work, many feel that their lives are useless, that they are doing nothing for the advancement of God's kingdom. If they could do some great thing how gladly they would undertake it! But because they can serve only in little things, they think themselves justified in doing nothing. In this they err. A man may be in the active service of God while engaged in the ordinary, everyday duties—while felling trees, clearing the ground, or following the plow. The mother who trains her children for Christ is as truly working for God as is the minister in the pulpit" (PK 219, 1917).

Self-Sacrificing Service
"Do not pass by the little things, and look for a large work. You might do successfully the small work, but fail utterly in attempting a large work and fall into discouragement. Take hold wherever you see that there is work to be done. Whether you are rich or poor, great or humble, God calls you into active service for Him. It will be by doing with your might what your hands find to do that you will develop talent and aptitude for the work, and it is by neglecting your daily opportunities that you become fruitless and withered. This is why there are so many fruitless trees in the garden of the Lord" (RH February 28, 1893).

"There is nothing, save the selfish heart of man, that lives unto itself. No bird that cleaves the air, no animal that moves upon the ground, but ministers to some other life. There is no leaf of the forest, or lowly blade of grass, but has its ministry. Every tree and shrub and leaf pours forth that element of life without which neither man nor animal could live; and man and animal in turn minister to the life of tree and shrub and leaf. The flowers breathe fragrance and unfold their beauty in blessing to the world. The sun sheds its light to gladden a thousand worlds. The ocean, itself the source of all our springs and fountains, receives the streams from every land, but takes to give. The mists ascending from its bosom fall in showers to water the earth, that it may bring forth and bud" (DA 20, 1898).

"Many, many, are approaching the day of God doing nothing, shunning responsibilities, and as the result, they are religious dwarfs. So far as work for God is concerned, the pages of their life history present a mournful blank. They are trees in the garden of God, but only cumberers of the ground, darkening with their unproductive boughs the ground which fruit-bearing trees might have occupied" (RH April 30, 1901).

"By the casting of grain into the earth, the Saviour represents His sacrifice for us. 'Except a corn of wheat fall into the ground and die,' He says, 'it abideth alone: but if it die, it bringeth forth much fruit.' John 12:24. Only through the sacrifice of Christ, the Seed, could fruit be brought forth for the kingdom of God. In accordance with the law of the vegetable kingdom, life is the result of His death.

"So with all who bring forth fruit as workers together with Christ: self-love, self-interest, must perish; the life must be cast into the furrow of the world's need. But the law of self-sacrifice is the law of self-preservation. The husbandman preserves his grain by casting it away. So the life that will be preserved is the life that is freely given in service to God and man.

"The seed dies, to spring forth into new life. In this we are taught the lesson of the resurrection. Of the human body laid away to molder in the grave, God has said: "It is sown in corruption; it is raised in incorruption: it is sown in dishonour; it is raised in glory: it is sown in weakness; it is raised in power.' 1 Corinthians 15:42, 43" (Ed 110, 1903).

"Trees that are crowded closely together do not grow healthfully and sturdily. The gardener transplants them that they may have room to develop. A similar work would benefit many of the members of large churches.

They need to be placed where their energies will be called forth in active Christian effort. They are losing their spiritual life, becoming dwarfed and inefficient, for want of self-sacrificing labor for others. Transplanted to some missionary field, they would grow strong and vigorous.

"But none need wait until called to some distant field before beginning to help others. Doors of service are open everywhere. All around us are those who need our help. The widow, the orphan, the sick and the dying, the heartsick, the discouraged, the ignorant, and the outcast are on every hand" (MH 152, 1905).

Tilling the Soil

"To every father and mother is committed a little plot of ground before their own door. It is their work to clear it from noxious weeds, and to mellow the soil that the precious seed may take root and flourish there. To do their work faithfully will be far more pleasing to God than to go on a mission to some foreign land, leaving the home field neglected. The work of Christian ministers and parents, should begin with their own children. Present to the church and to the world a well-disciplined family, and you present one of the strongest arguments in favor of Christianity" (ST November 10, 1881).

"'Ye are God's husbandry.' Will the students apply this lesson while they are working upon the land, tilling the soil, plowing and harrowing, putting all the skill they possess into the work of bringing the land into a condition where it will be fit for the planting of the seed, and the trees, preparatory for the harvest? Will they bear in mind that they are God's husbandry, a part of the Lord's farm, and that in this term of school there is a great deal of work to be done by those who are appointed to watch for souls as they that must give an account? There are hearts that need much more labor bestowed upon them because the soil has not been under the plow or the harrow. The hardened soil must be broken up and subdued, so that the word of God, the gospel seed, may find favorable soil for the production of a harvest.

"Let students call all their faculties of discernment to bear upon this subject. Let their skill interpret the figures used. The earth has to be worked to bring out its varied properties favorable to the growth of the seed and fruit. But the harvest will reward the painstaking efforts made in a supply of food for the necessities of man.

"The former and latter rains are needed. 'We are labourers together with God.' The Lord alone can give the precious former and latter rain.

The clouds, the sunshine, the dews at night—these are heaven's most precious provisions. But all these favors graciously bestowed of Heaven will prove of little worth to those who do not appropriate them by diligent, painstaking effort on their part. Personal efforts must be put forth in agriculture. There is plowing and replowing. Implements must be brought in and human skill must use them. The seed must be sown in its season. The laws which control seed time and harvest must be observed, else there will be no harvest.

"There must be an intelligent, harmonious co-operation of the divine and human. The working of the soil is a lesson book which, if read, will be of the greatest benefit to every student in our school. They may understand that surface work, haphazard half-effort, will reveal itself in the harvest to be garnered" (Ms182-1897).

"In felling the trees, in breaking the soil preparatory to sowing the seed, every toiler has a lesson to learn. And just in the way in which the land is treated, will be the spiritual work on the human heart. Those, who by vigilant, intelligent, persevering effort would be benefitted by the tilling of the soil, must break up the fallow ground of the heart, with the help of the softening, subduing influence of the Holy Spirit. Thus the cultivation of the soil will prove the education of the soul" (Lt3-1898).

"In tilling the soil, in disciplining and subduing the land, lessons may constantly be learned. No one would think of settling upon a raw piece of land, expecting it at once to yield a harvest. Earnestness, diligence, and persevering labor are to be put forth in treating the soil preparatory to sowing the seed. So it is in the spiritual work in the human heart. Those who would be benefited by the tilling of the soil must go forth with the word of God in their hearts. They will then find the fallow ground of the heart broken by the softening, subduing influence of the Holy Spirit. Unless hard work is bestowed on the soil, it will not yield a harvest. So with the soil of the heart: the Spirit of God must work upon it to refine and discipline it before it can bring forth fruit to the glory of God" (COL 88, 1900).

"The youth should be instructed in a similar way. From the tilling of the soil, lessons may constantly be learned. No one settles upon a raw piece of land with the expectation that it will at once yield a harvest. Diligent, persevering labor must be put forth in the preparation of the soil, the sowing of the seed, and the culture of the crop. So it must be in the spiritual sowing. The garden of the heart must be cultivated. The soil must be broken up by repentance. The evil growths that choke the good grain must be uprooted. As soil once overgrown with thorns can be reclaimed only by diligent labor, so the evil tendencies of the heart can be overcome only by earnest effort in the name and strength of Christ" (Ed 111, 1903).

> *"He who tills the soil is to make his work an object-lesson of the careful, thorough work which must be done in the culture of the soil of the heart."*

"He who tills the soil is to make his work an object-lesson of the careful, thorough work which must be done in the culture of the soil of the heart" (RH June 27, 1907).

"Administer the rules of the home in wisdom and love, not with a rod of iron. Children will respond with willing obedience to the rule of love. Commend your children whenever you can. Make their lives as happy as possible. Provide them with innocent amusements. Make the home a Bethel, a holy, consecrated place. Keep the soil of the heart mellow by the manifestation of love and affection, thus preparing it for the seed of truth. Remember that the Lord gives the earth not only clouds and rain, but the beautiful, smiling sunshine, causing the seed to germinate and the blossom to appear. Remember that children need not only reproof and correction, but encouragement and commendation, the pleasant sunshine of kind words" (CT 114, 1913).

Sowing the Seed

"Not only has the physical and mental health of children been endangered by being sent to school at too early a period, but they have been the losers in a moral point of view. They have had opportunities to become acquainted with children who were uncultivated in their manners. They were thrown into the society of the course and rough, who lie, swear, steal, and deceive, and who delight to impart their knowledge of vice to those younger than themselves. Young children, if left to themselves, learn the bad more readily than the good. Bad habits agree best with the natural heart, and the things which they see and hear in infancy and childhood are deeply imprinted upon their minds, and the bad seed sown in their young hearts will take root, and will become sharp thorns to wound the hearts of their parents.

"During the first six or seven years of a child's life, special attention should be given to its physical training, rather than the intellect. After this period, if the physical constitution is good, the education of both should receive attention. Infancy extends to the age of six or seven years. Up to this period, children should be left, like little lambs, to roam around the house and in the yards, skipping and jumping in the buoyancy of their spirits, free from care and trouble.

"Parents, especially mothers, should be the only teachers of such infant minds. They should not educate from books. The children will generally be inquisitive to learn the things of nature. They will ask questions in regard to the things they see and hear, and parents should improve the opportunity to instruct, and patiently answer, these little inquirers. They can in this manner get the advantage of the enemy, and fortify the minds of their children, by sowing good seed in their hearts, leaving no room for the bad to take root. The mother's loving instructions is what is needed by children of a tender age in the formation of character" (SA 132, 133, 1870).

"Children who are allowed to have their own way are not happy. The unsubdued heart has not within itself the elements of rest and contentment. The mind and heart must be disciplined and brought under proper restraint in order for the character to harmonize with the wise laws that govern our being. Restlessness and discontent are the fruits of indulgence and selfishness. The soil of the heart, like that of a garden, will produce weeds and brambles unless the seeds of precious flowers are planted there and receive care and cultivation. As in visible nature, so is it with the human soul" (4T 202, 1881).

"The mental and moral powers which God has given us do not constitute character. They are talents, which we are to improve, and which, if properly improved, will form a right character. A man may have precious seed in his hand, but that seed is not an orchard. The seed must be planted before it can become a tree. The mind is the garden, the character is the fruit. God has given us our faculties to cultivate and develop. Our own course determines our character. In training these powers so that they shall harmonize and form a valuable character, we have a work which no one but ourselves can do" (4T 606, 1881).

"Persons who indulge the habit of story-reading make no progress mentally or morally. The time so devoted is worse than wasted. The gospel seed that is sown in the heart remains unfruitful, or is choked by the weeds sown by such reading. Seed that does not spring up and bear fruit loses its power of germinating. The fig-tree which bore no fruit was doomed to be cut down, condemned as an encumbrance to the very soil it occupied. God requires healthy growth of every tree in the garden of the Lord. But story-reading dwarfs the intellect. Childhood and youth are the time to begin to store the mind, but not with the chips and dirt found in modern newspapers and sensational literature. The mind should be guarded carefully. Nothing should be allowed to enter that will harm or destroy its healthy vigor. But to prevent this, it should be preoccupied with good seed, which, springing to life, will bring forth fruit-bearing branches. If all kinds of seed are sown—good and bad indiscriminately—the mind's soil will be impoverished and demoralized by a wild and noxious growth. Weeds of every kind will flourish, and good seed attain no growth at all. A field left uncultivated speedily produces a rank growth of thistles and tangled vines, which exhaust the soil and are worthless to the owner. The ground is full of seeds blown and carried by the wind from every quarter; and if it is left uncultivated, they spring up to life spontaneously, choking every precious fruit-bearing plant that is struggling for existence. If the field were tilled and sown to grain, these valueless weeds would be extinguished, and could not flourish.

"The similarity between an uncultivated field and an untrained mind is striking. Children and youth already have in their minds and hearts corrupt seed, ready to spring up and bear its perverting harvest; and the greatest care and watchfulness are needed in cultivating and storing the mind with precious seeds of Bible truth. The children should be educated to reject trashy, exciting tales, and turn to sensible reading that will train their minds to be interested in Bible story, history, and arguments. If their imagination becomes excited by feeding it upon highly-wrought fictitious stories, they will have no desire to search the Scriptures or obtain a knowledge of truth to impart to others. Truth is what our youth should read and study, not fiction—truth to be practiced every day, that truth which Christ prayed might sanctify his disciples" (RH November 9, 1886).

"The best way to prevent the growth of evil is to preoccupy the soil. The greatest care and watchfulness is needed in cultivating the mind and sowing therein the precious seeds of Bible truth" (CTBH 125, 1890).

"In the home circle, at your neighbor's fireside, at the bedside of the sick, in a quiet way you may read the Scriptures and speak a word for Jesus and the truth. Precious seed may thus be sown, that will spring up and bring forth fruit after many days" (RH January 6, 1891).

"As parents educate their children according to God's order, teaching them both by precept and example to love and reverence God, to obey every word that proceedeth out of the mouth of God, they educate themselves, and strengthen their own souls in the love of Christ. He who teaches the lessons of Christ sows precious seed that not only reproduces itself in the hearts of those taught, but takes new root, and springs up afresh in the heart of the teacher. In presenting the truth so that it may be comprehended by undisciplined youthful minds, the parent or teacher finds that it has new power and vividness to his own soul. In seeking to impress its importance upon the conscience of the young, we realize its value to a greater extent than before, and better appreciate the divine character of our Redeemer. By dwelling upon the character of Christ, the teacher, beholding him, will become changed; he will catch his Spirit, and diffuse the light of the Sun of Righteousness, flashing the bright beams of Christ's righteousness into the minds of his pupils, and his own soul will be refreshed, and he will realize that whatsoever a man soweth, that shall he also reap" (ST April 27, 1891).

"Pharaoh had his sowing time, and he also had his reaping time. He sowed resistance and obstinacy. He sowed the seed in the soil. No new power was put into operation by God. The seed was left to spring up; the man was permitted to act out his true character. When the Lord sees unbelief in the heart against light and evidence, all he has to do is to let the human agent alone; for the seed put into the soil will bring forth seed after its kind. Many have been sowing the seed of unbelief, and if this seed is cultivated, it will produce a harvest that will not be so pleasant to reap as the seed is to sow. When Pharaoh refused to heed the messages and admonitions of God, and was not admonished by the first miracle that God worked to convince him, he was in a condition more easily to say, 'I will,' and 'I will not.' His independent resistance produced a harvest after its kind, and all the evidences that God gave to set his steps in the right path, only served to fasten him in unbelief and rebellion. He went on from one degree of resistance and wilful disobedience of God to another degree, just as the ungodly of all ages have done, and will do to the close of time, until he finally looked upon the dead face of his first-born. The character revealed by Pharaoh is similar to that of all the impenitent. God destroys no man; but after a time the wicked are given up to the destruction they have wrought for themselves" (YI November 30, 1893).

"In the physical world, the seed rewards the sower. First the blade appears, then the ear, then the corn in the ear, and then the harvest. There is an unseen agency at work from the time the seed is sown till the harvest is gathered. The dew, the blessed showers of heaven, which refresh, enrich, and nourish the tiny seed, the sunbeams, which bring life and warmth and gladness, these are all links in the chain of God's providence. The seed requires the richness of the soil, the air, the dew, the rain. The chain is forged by an unseen agency, even an omnipotent power, which works silently but effectually linking together the agencies which produce the harvest.

"Seed-sowing is a work which is done by the sower in faith. As it were, he casts away the seed, that there may be an ingathering, and he is rewarded by the harvest. Watch the worker preparing the soil for the seed. The slothful, careless worker only half prepares the soil, and the harvest always bears witness to the character of his work. He was not earnest and diligent in preparing the soil, and he finds nothing but disappointment in the harvest. He did not cultivate the ground thoroughly, and the result is that the crop is a failure, the seed is lost, and worthless harvest bears witness against him. The fruit gathered is not enough to repay him for his labors.

"So it is in spiritual things. From this we are to learn that the character of the worker is not always measured by the apparent result of his work, but by the faithful, honest work done. Our Saviour would have all study nature's laws; for they are a representation of the laws of grace. In all her works, nature is a teacher of spiritual things. As the ground is prepared for the seed, so the heart must be prepared for the seeds of truth. The weeds of sin and selfishness must be rooted out, for they will produce a harvest that the sower will not be desirous to gather. The good seed that is sown must be cultivated, and kept free from weeds. The soil of the heart must not be allowed to become hard. It must be warmed by the bright rays of the Sun of Righteousness. The light must not be quenched.

"He who gave the parable of the tiny mustard seed is the Sovereign of heaven, and the same laws that govern earthly seed-sowing and reaping govern the sowing of the seeds of truth.... In the gospel seed-sowing, the Word of God is to be communicated as truth; it is to be interwoven with the whole practical life" (Lt55-1897).

"After Christ's crucifixion, Jew and Greek, barbarian and Scythian, bond and free, would be able to understand his work, and to comprehend the words which upon this occasion he addressed to his disciples, 'Verily, verily, I say unto you,' he said, 'Except a corn of wheat fall into the ground and die, it abideth alone; but if it die, it bringeth forth much fruit.' Christ saw that the fallow ground of the heart must be broken up, the soil thoroughly worked, the good seed sown and carefully harrowed in. It was not pleasant for the disciples to submit to this. Many opposite influences had been at work confusing and beclouding their minds. But with what wisdom Christ presents his future, illustrating it by the things of nature, that the disciples might understand that the purpose of his mission was to be fulfilled by his death. 'Verily, verily, I say unto you,' he said. When Christ said, 'Verily, verily,' the disciples always understood that something of importance was to follow, and now, as they listened to his words, they saw divinity revealed in humanity. 'Verily, verily, I say unto you, Except a corn of wheat fall into the ground and die, it abideth alone; but if it die, it bringeth forth much fruit.' When the grain of wheat falls into the ground and dies, it springs up, and bears fruit. So the death of Christ would result in fruit for the kingdom of God. Life was to be the result of his death, in exact accordance with the law of the vegetable kingdom.

"Every harvest this lesson is repeated. Those who till the soil have the illustration of the Saviour's words ever before them. Year by year man preserves his grain by apparently throwing away his choicest sample. For a time this must be hidden under the furrow, to be watched over by the Lord. Then appears the blade, then the ear, and then the corn in the ear. But this development can not take place unless the grain is buried out of sight, hidden and, to all appearances, lost.

"The seed buried in the ground produces fruit, and in their turn the seeds of this fruit are planted. Thus the harvest is multiplied. So the death of Christ on the cross of Calvary will bear fruit unto eternal life. The contemplation of this sacrifice will be the glory of those who, as the fruit of it, will live through the eternal ages" (ST July 1, 1897).

"The cultivation of the soil, the sowing of the seed, the care bestowed on the seed by the sower, represent different stages of Christ's work for the soul. First appears the blade, then the ear, then the full corn in the ear.

"The man who sows seed apparently throws away that upon which he and his family depend for a living. But he is only giving up a present advantage for a much larger return. He throws the seed away that he may gather it again in an abundant harvest. By faith he may look forward to large returns....

"Christ seeks to lead the mind from the natural seed cast into the ground to the gospel seed, the sowing of which will result in bringing man back to his loyalty. The Saviour came to this world to sow the seed of truth. Like a sower in the field, he scattered the seeds of truth in the hearts of men.

"'He that received seed into the good ground is he that heareth the word, and understandeth it; which also beareth fruit, and bringeth forth, some an hundredfold, some sixty, some thirty.' Shall the expectation of the sower of the seed be disappointed? God forbid! for it is for the present and future good of the receiver that the seed sown be received into good ground. When it is received in faith, it will spring up and bear fruit.

"What does it mean to receive into the heart the good seed?—It means to receive the words of Christ. This is a remedy for sin. Some give the truth a partial reception, a half-sympathy, wishing at the same time they had never heard it. In such soil Satan sows his seed, and soon there is a growth of thorns, which chokes the good seed. But when the gospel seed is sown in soil that welcomes it, when it is incorporated with the life, direct and glorious results are seen,—results that testify to the infinite love of God and the transforming power of the gospel.

"It means much to receive the good seed. In Luke we read, 'That on the good ground are they, which in an honest and good heart, having heard the word, keep it, and bring forth fruit with patience.' An honest heart is a heart, which, when the light shines into it, acknowledges that sin is the transgression of the law. 'Take heed ... how ye hear,' said the Great Teacher. What will it avail to spend the life in self-deception? When truth is received into the heart, the tares growing there are uprooted. The appeals of God to the conscience are no longer turned aside as of no consequence.

"All who receive the word into good and honest hearts will bring forth fruit. In their hearts will spring up the precious fruits of the Spirit,—love, joy, peace, long-suffering, gentleness, goodness, faith, meekness, temperance" (YI August 16, 1900).

"In the earliest years of the child's life the soil of the heart is to be carefully prepared for the showers of God's grace. Then the seeds of truth are to be carefully sown and diligently tended. And God, who rewards every effort made in His name, will put life into the seed sown. There will appear first the blade, then the ear, then the full corn in the ear.

"Too often, because of the wicked neglect of parents, Satan sows his seeds in the hearts of children, and a harvest of shame and sorrow is borne. The world today is destitute of true goodness because parents have failed to gather their children to themselves in the home. They have not kept them from association with the careless and reckless. Therefore the children have gone forth into the world to sow the seeds of death" (ST September 25, 1901).

"When the tiller of the soil sows seed, he apparently throws away his grain. Parents may think that in teaching their children the principles of kindness and patience, they are throwing away their time and efforts. But if they are faithful in training their children, they will reap an abundant harvest as surely as will the one who sows good seed in his field" (Ms77-1902).

"The work of the sower is a work of faith. The mystery of the germination and growth of the seed he cannot understand; but he has confidence in the agencies by which God causes vegetation to flourish. He casts away the seed, expecting to gather it manyfold in an abundant harvest. So parents and teachers are to labor, expecting a harvest from the seed they sow.

"For a time the good seed may lie unnoticed in the heart, giving no evidence that it has taken root; but afterward, as the Spirit of God breathes on the soul, the hidden seed springs up, and at last brings forth fruit. In our lifework we know not which shall prosper, this or that. This question it is not for us to settle. 'In the morning sow thy seed, and in the evening withhold not thine hand.' Ecclesiastes 11:6. God's great covenant declares that 'while the earth remaineth, seedtime and harvest . . . shall not cease.' Genesis 8:22. In the confidence of this promise the husbandman tills and sows. Not less confidently are we, in the spiritual sowing, to labor, trusting His assurance: 'So shall my word be that goeth forth out of my mouth: it shall not return unto me void, but it shall accomplish that which I please, and it shall prosper in the thing whereto I sent it.' 'He that goeth forth and weepeth, bearing precious seed, shall doubtless come again with rejoicing, bringing his sheaves with him.' Isaiah 55:11; Psalm 126:6.

"The germination of the seed represents the beginning of spiritual life, and the development of the plant is a figure of the development of character. There can be no life without growth. The plant must either grow or die. As its growth is silent and imperceptible, but continuous, so is the growth of character. At every stage of development our life may be perfect; yet if God's purpose for us is fulfilled, there will be constant advancement....

"The wheat develops, 'first the blade, then the ear, after that the full corn in the ear.' Mark 4:28. The object of the husbandman in the sowing of the seed and the culture of the plant, is the production of grain—bread for the hungry, and seed for future harvests. So the divine Husbandman looks for a harvest. He is seeking to reproduce Himself in the hearts and lives of His followers, that through them He may be reproduced in other hearts and lives.

"The gradual development of the plant from the seed is an object lesson in child training. There is 'first the blade, then the ear, after that the full corn in the ear.' Mark 4:28. He who gave this parable created the tiny seed, gave it its vital properties, and ordained the laws that govern its growth. And the truths taught by the parable were made a reality in His own life. He, the Majesty of heaven, the King of glory, became a babe in Bethlehem, and for a time represented the helpless infant in its mother's care. In childhood He spoke and acted as a child, honoring His parents, and carrying out their wishes in helpful ways. But from the first dawning of intelligence He was constantly growing in grace and in a knowledge of truth.

"Parents and teachers should aim so to cultivate the tendencies of the youth that at each stage of life they may represent the beauty appropriate to that period, unfolding naturally, as do the plants in the garden.

"The little ones should be educated in childlike simplicity. They should be trained to be content with the small, helpful duties and the pleasures and experiences natural to their years. Childhood answers to the blade in the parable, and the blade has a beauty peculiarly its own. Children should not be forced into a precocious maturity, but as long as possible should retain the freshness and grace of their early years. The more quiet and simple the life of the child—the more free from artificial excitement and the more in harmony with nature—the more favorable it is to physical and mental vigor and to spiritual strength" (Ed 105–107, 1903).

> *"The more quiet and simple the life of the child—the more free from artificial excitement and the more in harmony with nature—the more favorable it is to physical and mental vigor and to spiritual strength."*

"The harvest is a reproduction of the seed sown. Every seed yields fruit after its kind. So it is with the traits of character we cherish. Selfishness, self-love, self-esteem, self-indulgence, reproduce themselves, and the end is wretchedness and ruin. 'He that soweth to his flesh shall of the flesh reap corruption; but he that soweth to the Spirit shall of the Spirit reap life everlasting.' Galatians 6:8. Love, sympathy, and kindness yield fruitage of blessing, a harvest that is imperishable.

"In the harvest the seed is multiplied. A single grain of wheat, increased by repeated sowings, would cover a whole land with golden sheaves. So widespread may be the influence of a single life, of even a single act.

"What deeds of love the memory of that alabaster box broken for Christ's anointing has through the long centuries prompted! What countless gifts that contribution, by a poor unnamed widow, of 'two mites, which make a farthing' (Mark 12:42), has brought to the Saviour's cause!

"The lesson of seed sowing teaches liberality. 'He which soweth sparingly shall reap also sparingly; and he which soweth bountifully shall reap also bountifully.' 2 Corinthians 9:6.

"The Lord says, 'Blessed are ye that sow beside all waters.' Isaiah 32:20. To sow beside all waters means to give wherever our help is needed. This will not tend to poverty. 'He which soweth bountifully shall reap also bountifully.' By casting it away the sower multiplies his seed. So by imparting we increase our blessings. God's promise assures a sufficiency, that we may continue to give.

"More than this: as we impart the blessings of this life, gratitude in the recipient prepares the heart to receive spiritual truth, and a harvest is produced unto life everlasting....

"As parents and teachers try to teach these lessons, the work should be made practical. Let the children themselves prepare the soil and sow the seed. As they work, the parent or teacher can explain the garden of the heart, with the good or bad seed sown there, and that as the garden must be prepared for the natural seed, so the heart must be prepared for the seed of truth. As the seed is cast into the ground, they can teach the lesson of Christ's death; and as the blade springs up, the truth of the resurrection. As the plant grows, the correspondence between the natural and the spiritual sowing may be continued" (Ed 109–111, 1903).

"The best way to prevent the growth of evil is to preoccupy the soil. Instead of recommending your children to read *Robinson Crusoe*, or fascinating stories of real life, such as *Uncle Tom's Cabin*, open the Scriptures to them, and spend some time each day in reading and studying God's word. The mental tastes must be disciplined and educated with the greatest care. Parents must begin early to unfold the Scriptures to the expanding minds of their children, that proper habits of thought may be formed.

"No effort should be spared to establish right habits of study. If the mind wanders, bring it back. If the intellectual and moral tastes have been perverted by overwrought and exciting tales of fiction, so that there is a disinclination to apply the mind, there is a battle to be fought to overcome this habit. A love for fictitious reading should be overcome at once. Rigid rules should be enforced to hold the mind in the proper channel.

"Between an uncultivated field and an untrained mind there is a striking similarity. In the minds of children and youth the enemy sows tares, and unless parents keep watchful guard, these will spring up to bear their evil fruit. Unceasing care is needed in cultivating the soil of the mind and sowing it with the precious seed of Bible truth. Children should be taught to reject trashy, exciting tales, and to turn to sensible reading, which will lead the mind to take an interest in Bible story, history, and argument. Reading that will throw light upon the Sacred Volume and quicken the desire to study it is not dangerous, but beneficial" (CT 136, 1913).

"We are living in an unfortunate age of the young. The prevailing influence in society is in favor of allowing the youth to follow the natural turn of their own minds. If their children are very wild, parents flatter themselves that when they are older and reason for themselves they will leave off their wrong habits and become useful men and women. What a mistake! For years they permit an enemy to sow the garden of the heart, and suffer wrong principles to grow and strengthen, seeming not to discern the hidden dangers and the fearful ending of the path that seems to them the way of happiness. In many cases all the labor afterward bestowed upon these youth will avail nothing" (CT 325, 1913).

Cultivation (Weeding)

"As you cultivate your vegetables and flowers, and remove the weeds and prune from them the lifeless branches, bear in mind this is the work God is doing for you if he loves you. As you remove everything unsightly, and injurious to your plants, that nothing but the beautiful may appear, remember that just so God is doing with your human garden. He would discipline you, and would root out all the weeds, and all corruption and vileness, that you may possess a symmetrical character, and be free from evil habits, that you may not become sour, distrustful, and gloomy" (HR June 1, 1871).

"These persons could cultivate and enrich the soil of their hearts, if they would, so that the truth would take deeper hold; but this involves too much patience and self-denial. It costs them too much effort to make a radical change in their lives. They are easily offended by reproof, and ready to say with the disciples who left Jesus, 'This is a hard saying; who can hear it?' 'And these are they likewise which are sown on stony ground; who, when they have heard the word, immediately receive it with gladness; and have no root in themselves, and so endure but for a time: afterward, when affliction or persecution ariseth for the word's sake, immediately they are offended.'

"Jesus represents the seed as falling into neglected borders and patches covered with rank weeds which choke the precious plants that spring up among them; they grow sickly and perish. Many hearts respond to the voice of truth, but they do not properly receive and cherish it. They give it a place in the soil of the natural heart, without preparing the ground and rooting out the poisonous weeds that flourish there, and watching every hour in order to destroy them should they again appear. The cares of life, the fascination of riches, the longing for forbidden things, crowd out the love of righteousness before the good seed can bear fruit. Pride, passion, self-love, and love of the world, with envy and malice, are no companions for the truth of God. As it is necessary thoroughly to cultivate the soil that has once been overgrown with weeds, so it is necessary for the Christian to be diligent in exterminating the faults that threaten his eternal ruin. Patient, earnest effort in the name and strength of Jesus, can alone remove the evil tendencies of the natural heart. But those who have allowed their faith to be overcome by the growth of Satan's influences, fall into a worse state than that which they occupied before they heard the words of life. 'And these are they which are sown among thorns; such as hear the word, and the cares of this world, and the deceitfulness of riches, and the lusts of other things entering in, choke the word, and it becometh unfruitful.'

"Few hearts are like the good soil, well-cultivated, and receive the seeds of truth and bring forth abundant fruit to the glory of God. But Jesus finds some earnest Christians, rich in good works and sincere in their endeavors. 'And these are they which are sown on good ground; such as hear the word, and receive it, and bring forth fruit, some thirtyfold, some sixty, and some an hundred.' (2SP 239, 240, 1877).

"Fathers and mothers too often leave their children to choose for themselves their amusements, their companions, and their occupation. The result is such as might reasonably be expected. Leave a field uncultivated, and it will grow up to thorns and briers. You will never see a lovely flower or a choice shrub peering above the unsightly, poisonous weeds. The worthless bramble will grow luxuriantly without thought or care, while plants that are valued for use or beauty require thorough culture. Thus it is with our youth. If right habits are formed, and right principles established, there is earnest work to be done. If wrong habits are corrected, diligence and perseverance are required to accomplish the task" (RH September 13, 1881).

"The very beginnings of evil, the first manifestations of insubordination, should be resolutely checked. The indulgence of appetite and passion should be restrained with earnestness and decision. When parents neglect this work, they permit thorns and briers to occupy the heart-gardens which God has commanded them to sow with precious seed, and to till with care, that a harvest may be brought forth unto eternal life. God will surely visit the transgressors with judgment. Both parents and children must reap the harvest sown" (ST December 8, 1881).

"I address myself to both yourself and your wife. My position in the cause and work of God demands of me an expression in matters of discipline. Your example in your own domestic affairs will do a great injury to the cause of God. The gospel field is the world. You wish to sow the field with gospel truth, waiting for God to water the seed sown that it may bring forth fruit. You have entrusted to you a little plot of ground, but your own dooryard is left to grow up with brambles and thorns, while you are engaged in weeding others' gardens. This is not a small work, but one of great moment. You are preaching the gospel to others; practice it yourself at home. You are indulging the whims and passions of a perverse child, and by so doing are cultivating traits of character which God hates and which make the child unhappy. Satan takes advantage of your neglect, and he controls the mind. You have a work to do to show that you understand the duties devolving upon a Christian father in molding the character of your child after the divine Pattern. Had you commenced this work in her infancy, it would be easy now, and the child would be far happier. But under your discipline the will and perversity of the child have all the while been strengthening. Now it will require greater severity, and more constant, persevering effort, to undo what you have been doing. If you cannot manage one little child that it is your special duty to control, you will be deficient in wisdom in managing the spiritual interests of the church of Christ" (4T 381, 1881).

"The human mind is represented by the rich soil of a garden. Unless it shall receive proper cultivation, it will be overgrown with the weeds and briers of ignorance. The mind and heart need culture daily, and neglect will be productive of evil. The more natural ability God has bestowed upon an individual, the greater the improvement he is required to make, and the greater his responsibility to use his time and talents for the glory of God. The mind must not remain dormant. If it is not exercised in the acquisition of knowledge, there will be a sinking into ignorance, superstition, and fancy. If the intellectual faculties are not cultivated as they should be to glorify God, they will become powerful aids in leading to perdition" (4T 442, 1881).

Sometimes parents wait for the Lord to do the very work that he has given them to do. Instead of restraining and controlling their children as they should, they pet and indulge them, and gratify their whims and desires. When these children go out from their early homes, it is with characters deformed by selfishness, with ungoverned appetites, with strong self-will; they are destitute of courtesy or respect for their parents, and do not love religious truth or the worship of God. They have grown up with traits that are a life-long curse to themselves and to others. Home is made anything but happy if the evil weeds of dissension, selfishness, envy, passion, and sullen stubbornness are left to flourish in the neglected garden of the soul" (ST January 31, 1884).

"We are living amid the perils of the last days, and we should guard every avenue by which Satan can approach us with his temptations. A fatal delusion seizes those who have had great light and precious opportunities, but who have not walked in the light nor improved the opportunities God has given them. Darkness comes upon them; they fail to make Christ their strength, and fall an easy prey to the snares of the deceiver. A mere assent to the truth will never save a soul from death. We must be sanctified through the truth; every defect of character must be overcome, or it will overcome us, and become a controlling power for evil. Commence without a moment's delay to root out every pernicious weed from the garden of the heart; and, through the grace of Christ, allow no plants to flourish there but such as will bear fruit unto eternal life" (RH June 3, 1884).

"There is earnest work to be done in this age, and parents should educate their children to share in it. If you would educate your children to serve God and do good in the world, make the Bible your textbook. Whatever else is taught in the home or at school, the Bible, as the great educator, should stand first. If it is given this place, God is honored, and he will work for you in the conversion of your children. There is a rich mine of truth and beauty in this holy book, and parents have themselves to blame if they do not make it intensely interesting to their children. The first and most precious knowledge is the knowledge of Christ; and wise parents will keep this fact ever before the minds of their children. Bible rules must be written on the heart. Bible rules must be carried into the every-day life. The Christian may lift up his soul to God for strength and grace amid every discouragement. Kind words, pleasant looks, a cheerful countenance, throw a charm around the Christian that makes his influence almost irresistible. It is the religion of Christ in the heart that causes the words issuing therefrom to be gentle, and the demeanor condescending, even to those in the humblest walks of life. The words we speak, our daily deportment, are the fruit growing upon the tree. If the fruit is sour and unpalatable, the roots of that tree are not drawing nourishment from a pure source. If our affections are brought into harmony with our Saviour, if our characters are meek and lowly, we evidence that our life is hid with Christ in God; and we shall leave behind us a bright track. Christian politeness should be cultivated by daily practice. That unkind word should be left unspoken, that selfish disregard for the happiness of others should give place to sympathy and thoughtfulness. True courtesy, blended with truth and justice, will make the life not only useful but fragrant. Home is made anything but happy, if the evil weeds of dissension, selfishness, envy, passion, and sullen stubbornness are left to flourish in the neglected garden of the soul" (HM June 1, 1889).

"Those who take it upon themselves to watch their neighbor's garden instead of weeding their own plot of ground will surely find their own gardens so grown up to weeds that every precious plant will be crowded out" (5T 285, 1889).

"There are many who think they have a burden for souls, who talk in public of how much they love God, and yet they see no necessity of weeding the garden of the heart, see no necessity of letting the light of the Sun of Righteousness in to nourish the plants that God has planted. Such do not know Jesus; they do not know what it means to be a Christian. It takes earnestness, patience, prayer, and genuine faith to war successfully against evil dispositions. But it is necessary that even the thoughts should be brought into subjection to Christ" (Lt18b-1891).

"The plant of love must be carefully nourished, else it will die. Every good principle must be cherished if we would have it thrive in the soul. That which Satan plants in the heart,—envy, jealousy, evil surmising, evil speaking, impatience, prejudice, selfishness, covetousness, and vanity,—must be uprooted. If these evil things are allowed to remain in the soul, they will bear fruit by which many shall be defiled. Oh, how many cultivate the poisonous plants, that kill out the precious fruits of love and defile the soul! Some of these who cherish evil, think they have a burden for souls. They make public profession of their love to God, and yet see no necessity for weeding the garden of the heart, for uprooting every unsightly, unholy weed, for letting the beams of the Sun of Righteousness shine into the soul temple. They do not know Jesus. They have no knowledge of what it is to be a practical Christian, that is, to be Christlike" (ST November 14, 1892).

"God does not generally work miracles to advance His truth. If the husbandman neglects to cultivate the soil after sowing his seed, God works no miracle to counteract the sure result of neglect. In the harvest he will find his field barren. God works according to great principles which he has presented to the human family, and it is our part to mature wise plans, and set in operation the means whereby God shall bring about certain results" (RH September 28, 1897).

"If properly managed, the cultivation of the soil will not be considered drudgery. The work is to be done intelligently. Study to begin the training process in the work done on the land. That which is done should be explained to the worker, just as in any trade. And the blessing of the Lord will rest upon those who are working upon the land, and learning spiritual lessons from nature. In cultivating the soil, the student little knows what treasures will open up before him. While he is not to despise the instruction he may gather from minds that have had an experience, and from the information that intelligent men can impart, he should gather lessons for himself. This is part of his education" (Lt3-1898).

"The Lord has entrusted to parents a solemn, sacred work. They are to cultivate carefully the soil of the heart. Thus they may be laborers together with God. He expects them to guard and tend carefully the garden of their children's hearts. They are to sow the good seed, weeding out every unsightly plant. Every defect in character, every fault in the disposition, needs to be cut away; for if allowed to remain, these will mar the beauty of the character" (ST August 23, 1899).

"In the beginning the Lord enjoined upon man the cultivation of the earth. This work was made much harder because of the transgression of the law of God. By transgressing man worked against his own present and eternal good. The earth was cursed because through disobedience man gave Satan opportunity to sow in the human heart the seeds of evil. The ground that in the beginning produced only good began to produce tares, and their growth called for continual warfare.... As he cultivates the soil, man is to see reflected as in a mirror the work of God upon the human soul" (Lt5-1900).

"If you cultivate faithfully the garden of your soul, you will not boast; for it is God that worketh in you. He is making you a laborer together with himself. Receive the grace and instruction of Christ, that you may impart to others a knowledge of how to cultivate the precious plants. Thus we may extend the Lord's vineyard. The Lord is watching for evidences of our faith and love and patience. He looks to see if we are using every spiritual advantage to become skillful workers before we enter the paradise of God, the Eden home from which Adam and Eve were excluded by transgression. It is ours to have that beautiful garden to cultivate under the supervision of God. Eden restored,—how beautiful it will be! how pleasant will be our employment! Then let us prove our industry by doing faithful work. Do not say, with the faithless sinner, 'I will not,' nor with the untrue son, 'I go, sir,' and go not; but at the call of Christ let us engage in sincere service" (YI April 26, 1900).

"Parents should be constant learners in the school of Christ. They need freshness and power, that with the simplicity of Christ they may teach the younger members of God's family the knowledge of His will. Line upon line, precept upon precept, they are to reiterate His lessons. They are to be diligent students of the Bible, that they may be apt in the tillage of the garden of the heart. With persevering effort they are to cultivate the hearts of the children placed in their care; and God will help them in every faithful, patient effort....

"In the cultivation of the garden of the heart, the efforts of parents must be unceasing, or unsightly weeds will spring up and choke the good seed. The weeds which spring up, the natural imperfections which appear, must be removed. Day by day parents are to watch vigilantly and correct wisely, insisting upon prompt obedience" (ST September 25, 1901).

In the cultivation of the soil the thoughtful worker will find that treasures little dreamed of are opening up before him. No one can succeed in agriculture or gardening without attention to the laws involved. The special needs of every variety of plant must be studied. Different varieties require different soil and cultivation, and compliance with the laws governing each is the condition of success. The attention required in transplanting, that not even a root fiber shall be crowded or misplaced, the care of the young plants, the pruning and watering, the shielding from frost at night and sun by day, keeping out weeds, disease, and insect pests, the training and arranging, not only teach important lessons concerning the development of character, but the work itself is a means of development. In cultivating carefulness, patience, attention to detail, obedience to law, it imparts a most essential training. The constant contact with the mystery of life and the loveliness of nature, as well as the tenderness called forth in ministering to these beautiful objects of God's creation, tends to quicken the mind and refine and elevate the character; and the lessons taught prepare the worker to deal more successfully with other minds" (Ed 111, 1903).

"Instead of finding fault with others, let us be critical with ourselves. Every one should inquire, Is my heart right before God? Am I glorifying my Heavenly Father? If you have cherished a wrong spirit, banish it from the soul. Eradicate from your heart everything that is of a defiling nature. Pluck up every root of bitterness, lest others be contaminated by the baleful influence. Do not allow one poisonous plant to remain in the soil of your heart. Root it out this very hour and cultivate in its stead the plant of love. Let Jesus be enshrined in the soul-temple" (RH February 25, 1904).

"Let the farm be diligently worked.... The same faithful work needed in the cultivation of the land is needed in soul-culture" (Lt129-1905).

"If a field is left uncultivated, a crop of weeds is sure to appear. So it is with children. If the soil of the heart is uncultivated, Satan sows his seeds of anger and hatred, selfishness and pride, and they quickly spring up, to bear a harvest that parents reap with bitter regret. Too late they see their terrible mistake. The wrong they have done can never be wholly undone. Even if the child, by patient, untiring care, is at last won to the Saviour, his character will always bear the marks of Satan's seed-sowing" (RH January 24, 1907).

The Fruit

"When the farmers seek to recommend or exhibit their products, they do not gather up the poorest but the best specimens. Women possess a zeal to bring the very best golden lumps of butter, molded and prettily stamped. Men bring the best yield of vegetables of every kind. The very best and most attractive fruit is brought, and their appearance does the skillful workers credit. The variety of fruits—the apples, peaches, apricots, oranges, lemons, and plums—all these are very attractive, and make those who look upon the fruit from the orchards and gardens, desire to be in the country where they can till the soil.

"No one would bring the most dwarfed specimens, but the very choicest which the land can produce. And why should not Christians living in these last days reveal the most attractive fruit in unselfish actions? Why should not the fruit of the commandment keeping people of God appear in the very best representation of good works? Their words, their deportment, their dress, should bear fruit of the very best quality. By their fruits, Christ said, ye shall know them" (Ms70-1897).

Agriculture in the Last Days

"The greater the length of time the earth has lain under the curse, the more difficult has it been for man to cultivate it, and make it productive. As the soil has become more barren, and double labor has had to be expended upon it, God has raised up men with inventive faculties to construct implements to lighten labor on the land groaning under the curse. But God has not been in all man's inventions. Satan has controlled the minds of men to a great extent, and has hurried men to new inventions which has led them to forget God" (4aSG 155, 1864).

"The time is not far distant when the laws against Sunday labor will be more stringent, and an effort should be made to secure grounds away from the cities, where fruits and vegetables can be raised. Agriculture will open resources for self-support, and various other trades also could be learned. This real, earnest work calls for strength of intellect as well as of muscle. Method and tact are required even to raise fruits and vegetables successfully. And habits of industry will be found an important aid to the youth in resisting temptation" (Ms8a-1894).

"I then presented before them [attendees of the Australian Union Conference] the necessity of those who were crowded into the cities procuring land in localities far from the cities, where they could cultivate the soil. The cities were growing more and more as was the earth before the flood, and more and more as Sodom, preparing for the fate of Sodom" (Lt84-1898).

"This earth has been cursed because of sin, and in these last days vermin of every kind will multiply. These pests must be killed, or they will annoy and torment and even kill us, and destroy the work of our hands and the fruit of our land. In places there are ants [termites] which entirely destroy the woodwork of houses. Should not these be destroyed? Fruit trees must be sprayed that the insects which would spoil the fruit may be killed. God has given us a part to act, and this part we must act with faithfulness. Then we can leave the rest with the Lord" (Ms70-1901).

"To parents who are living in the cities the Lord is sending the warning cry, Gather your children into your own houses; gather them away from those who are disregarding the commandments of God, who are teaching and practicing evil. Get out of the cities as fast as possible.

"Parents can secure small homes in the country, with land for cultivation where they can have orchards and where they can raise vegetables and small fruits to take the place of flesh meat which is so corrupting to the lifeblood coursing through the veins. On such places the children will not be surrounded with the corrupting influences of city life. God will help His people to find such homes outside of the cities" (Ms133-1902).

"The time has come, when, as God opens the way, families should move out of the cities. The children should be taken into the country. The parents should get as suitable a place as their means will allow. Though the dwelling may be small, yet there should be land in connection with it, that may be cultivated. Some families who have been separated may be united in such places" (Ms50-1903).

> *"Again and again the Lord has instructed that our people are to take their families away from the cities, into the country, where they can raise their own provisions."*

"Again and again the Lord has instructed that our people are to take their families away from the cities, into the country, where they can raise their own provisions; for in the future the problem of buying and selling will be a very serious one. We should now begin to heed the instruction given us over and over again: Get out of the cities into rural districts, where the houses are not crowded closely together, and where you will be free from the interference of enemies....

"Many do not see the importance of having land to cultivate, and of raising fruit and vegetables, that their tables may be supplied with these things. I am instructed to say to every family and every church, God will bless you when you work out your own salvation with fear and trembling, fearing lest, by unwise treatment of the body, you will mar the Lord's plan for you" (Lt5-1904).

"We need a genuine education in the art of cooking. Instead of multiplying our restaurants, it will be better to form classes where you may teach the people how to make good bread and how to put together the ingredients to make healthful food combinations from the grains and the vegetables. Such an education will assist in creating a desire among our people to move out of the cities, to secure land in the country, where they can raise their own fruit and vegetables. Then they can care for their gardens, and their food will not come to them half spoiled and decayed" (Ms150-1905).

"Parents, time is short; you have none to waste. Teach your children to be the Lord's little missionaries, His helping hand in doing a good work in the earth. Many a child who lives out of the city can have a little plot of land where he can learn to garden. He can be taught to make this a means of securing money to give to the cause of God. Both boys and girls can engage in this work; and it will, if they are rightly instructed, teach them the value of money and how to economize. It is possible for the children, besides raising money for missionary purposes, to be able to help in buying their own clothes, and they should be encouraged to do this" (Lt356-1907).

"There is plenty of land lying waste in the South that might have been improved as the land about the Madison school has been improved. The time is soon coming when God's people, because of persecution, will be scattered in many countries. Those who have received an all-round education will have the advantage wherever they are. The Lord reveals divine wisdom in thus leading His people to the training of all their faculties and capabilities for the work of disseminating truth" (Lt32a-1908).

"Do not consider it a privation when you are called to leave the cities and move out into country places. Here there await rich blessings for those who will grasp them. By beholding the scenes of nature, the works of the Creator, by studying God's handiwork, imperceptibly you will be changed into the same image" (Ms85-1908).

"The time will come that all who live upon the earth will need to understand the cultivating of the land and the building of houses and varied kinds of business" (Ms126-1908).

Ellen White Led by Example

The Early Years
"My mother was a great lover of flowers, and took much pleasure in cultivating them, and thus making her home attractive and pleasant for her children. But our garden had never before looked so lovely to me as upon the day of our return [from a Methodist camp meeting ca. 1840 where Ellen tasted the new birth experience]. I recognized an expression of the love of Jesus in every shrub, bud, and flower. These things of beauty seemed to speak in mute language of the love of God.

"There was a beautiful pink flower in the garden called the Rose of Sharon. I remember approaching it and touching the delicate petals reverently; they seemed to possess a sacredness in my eyes. My heart overflowed with tenderness and love for these beautiful creations of God. I could see divine perfection in the flowers that adorned the earth. God tended them, and his all-seeing eye was upon them. He had made them and called them good. 'Ah,' thought I, 'If he so loves and cares for the flowers that he has decked with beauty, how much more tenderly will he guard the children who are formed in his image.' I repeated softly to myself, 'I am a child of God, his loving care is around me, I will be obedient and in no way displease him, but will praise his dear name and love him always.'" (LS80 144, 1880).

[Battle Creek, MI] "Monday, April 11, 1859. Spent most of the day making a garden for my children. Feel willing to make home as pleasant for them as I can, that home may be the pleasantest place of any to them" (Ms6-1859).

"Dear little Willie: We have not forgotten you, my dear boy. When we see other little children around, we long to get our little Willie in our arms again, and press his little soft cheek, and receive his kiss. In about five weeks we shall be at home again, and then, Willie, we will work in the garden, and tend the flowers and plant the seeds. You must be a good, sweet, little boy, and love to obey Jenny and Lucinda" (Lt3-1860).

"Dear children, I do not write merely for your amusement, but for your improvement. Learn where you fail, and then commence the work of reform in earnest. You must learn order. Have set hours to work in the garden, set hours in the heat of the day to arrange your garden seeds, set hours to read and improve your minds. Spend no precious moments in bickerings and finding fault with each other.... Your affectionate Mother" (AY 70, 1864).

"We returned north, and on our way held a good meeting at West Windsor, and after reaching home held meetings at Fairplains and Orleans, and also gave some attention to the matter of building, planted our garden, and set out grapes, blackberries, raspberries, and strawberries" (1T 592, 1868).

"I think it is the best thing you can do, to have some knowledge of farming....

"Again, we think more of your health than means or property. We want you to have active exercise on a farm this summer. We want you to become a devoted Christian; obtain an experience in the things of God" (Lt4-1869, to Edson White).

"We spent a very pleasant week in Washington [Iowa]. I wrote more in one week than I have written in six weeks at Battle Creek. We had no interruptions, although I have not spent all the time in writing. I walked in the beautiful garden, worked in the field weeding out strawberries until I become so lame I could not move without much pain" (Lt9-1870).

"Spring has gone, and summer opens before us. The fragrant blossoms, beautifying the boughs of the apple, peach, and cherry, no longer delight the eye, and their sweet fragrance is not borne to us on the breeze. These useful trees, although they now make no display, are not resting from their labor. They are preparing to adorn their branches with a rich harvest of fruit by and by, to reward our care and patience.

"Our flower gardens are now repaying us for the attention and labor we have bestowed upon them. The flowering shrubs that live through winter, are many of them pleasing the eye by putting out their buds and blossoms. The seeds we have carefully put into the earth are making their appearance, while others are thirsting for the gentle showers to awaken them to life. All the beautiful in nature seems to be upon a strife to see which can vie with the other in contributing to our pleasure and happiness, by their buds and blossoms of every hue" (HR June 1, 1871).

"Last evening the two Marys went with me to Brooklyn [CA] for a few flower roots for our garden. Sister Grover gave us as many as we could carry.... We set out our flowers by moonlight and with the aid of a lamp" (Lt3-1876).

> *We set out our flowers by moonlight and with the aid of a lamp"*

"We came home and I set out my things in my garden of [the] new house by moonlight and by the aid of lamplight. The two Marys tried to have me wait till morning, but I would not listen to them. We had a beautiful shower last night. I was glad then I persevered in setting out my plants" (Lt4-1876, both to James White).

"Will you send me one of my straw hats by Frank Patten? If you could dry a few peony roots and let her take them in her trunk, and send a few slips of Queen of Prairie and a few choice seeds, as summer greens and pansy seeds, I should like some of these things so much. Send me verbena seeds. See if Sister Chapman has these things.

"In our old place, in the field which we sold, I wish you could send a slip of snowballs and a trumpet vine. These would take but little space and if you could send them I could have something new here [Oakland, CA] which they have not" (Lt61-1876).

"Father has excellent health. He has worked hard on the place here [MI]; put in more than one acre of strawberries, some raspberries, more than an acre of potatoes, several acres of corn, fifty hard maples, many peach trees, pear trees, and two long rows of pie plant. I have been gathering up shrubs and flowers until we have quite a garden. Peonies, I have a large number of them; hope to get California pinks. I want to get some of that green bordering we get from Sister Rollin. How can I get it? I wish I had some seeds from California" (Lt4a-1881, to "Children").

[Healdsburg, CA] "We have in about one thousand grapes; have one thousand more to set. We have beans, corn, and other things planted for [the] garden. Not but few peas yet. Have plenty more to plant" (Lt4-1882).

"While waiting for Brother Harmon, Brother Roberts and I went into the Italian garden, one mile from Brother Roberts' [place], and dug up more strawberry plants. I found a large quantity of little beets; brought some home to transplant. Found many spinach plants which we will transplant....

"Brother Ballou prepared ground for the plants, and I have now all the strawberry bed I care for. I helped Roberts last Tuesday plant parsnips, cabbage seed, carrot seed and beet seed. We shall have a garden if the Lord favors us" (Lt8-1882).

"I know by experience the value of an outdoor life to those who are sick. Years ago, when living in Battle Creek, it was thought that I was dying. My friends said to my husband, 'Brother White, your wife will not live long.' 'Yes,' he answered one day, 'she would not live long if she remained here; but she is going away with me today.' Accompanied by my son Willie, we started in a phaeton for Greenville eighty miles north. As I could not sit up during the journey, I knelt on two cushions placed on the bottom of the phaeton, leaning my head on my husband's knees.

"After reaching Greenville, my husband took me out to a strawberry bed and allowed me to work in the soil. He arranged everything for my convenience and brought out an easy chair. I was to set out the strawberry plants. This exercise in the open air seemed to take the poison out of my system. For some time I had coughed constantly—day and night. It seemed as if it were impossible to cease coughing. I could sleep but little. But after beginning to work in the soil, my cough left me. Although this outdoor exercise was the only medicine I took, I was rapidly restored to health.

"Many years ago, while my husband was bearing heavy responsibilities in Battle Creek, the strain began to tell on him. His health failed rapidly. Finally he broke down in mind and body and was unable to do anything. My friends said to me, 'Mrs. White, your husband cannot live.' I determined to remove him to a place more favorable for his recovery. His mother said, 'Ellen, you must remain and take care of your family.' 'Mother,' I replied, 'I will never allow that masterly brain to fail entirely. I will work with God, and

God will work with me, to save my husband's brain.'

"In order to obtain means for our journey, I pulled up my rag carpets and sold them. Years before, when I was making these carpets, Father used to come in and begin to sing, 'There'll be no rag carpets over there.' But afterward, when the time came that I sold these carpets to get money to take him into the country, I told him that it was these very rag carpets that made it possible for me to take him to a place where he could recover. With the money secured by the sale of the carpets, I bought a covered wagon and prepared for the journey, placing in the wagon a mattress for Father to lie on. Accompanied by Willie, a mere lad eleven years of age, we started for Wright, Michigan.

"While on the journey, Willie tried to put the bits into the mouth of one of the horses but found that he could not. I said to my husband, 'Put your hand on my shoulder, and come and put the bits in.' He said that he did not see how he could. 'Yes, you can,' I replied. 'Get right up and come.' He did so and succeeded in putting the bits in. Then he knew that he would have to do it the next time, too. Constantly I kept my husband working at such little things. I would not allow him to remain quiet but tried to keep him active. This is the plan that physicians and helpers in our sanitariums should pursue. Lead the patients along step by step, step by step, keeping their minds so busily occupied that they have no time to brood over their own condition....

"Daily my husband went out for a walk. In the winter a terrible snowstorm came, and Father thought he could not go out in the storm and snow. I went to Brother Root and said, 'Brother Root, have you a [spare] pair of boots?' 'Yes,' he answered. 'I should be glad to borrow them this morning,' I said. Putting on the boots and starting out, I tracked a quarter of a mile in the deep snow. On my return, I asked my husband to take a walk. He said he could not go out in such weather. 'O yes, you can,' I replied. 'Surely you can step in my tracks.' He was a man who had great respect for women; and when he saw my tracks, he thought that if a woman could walk in that snow, he could. That morning he took his usual walk.

"In the spring there were fruit trees to be set out and a garden to be made. 'Willie,' I said, 'please buy three hoes and three rakes. Be sure to buy three of each.' When he brought them to me, I told him to take one of the hoes, and Father another. Father objected, but took one. Taking one myself, we began to work; and although I blistered my hands, I led them in the hoeing. Father could not do much, but he went through the motions.

"It was by such methods as these that I tried to co-operate with God in restoring my husband to health. And oh, how the Lord blessed us! I always took my husband with me when I went out driving. And I took him with me when I went to preach at any place....

"After eighteen months of constant co-operation with God in the effort to restore my husband to health, I took him home again. Presenting him to his parents, I said, 'Father, Mother, here is your son.' 'Ellen,' said his Mother, 'you have no one but God and yourself to thank for this wonderful restoration. Your energies have accomplished it.' After his recovery, my husband lived for a number of years, during which time he did the best work of his life. Did not those added years of usefulness repay me manyfold for the eighteen months of painstaking care? I have given you this brief recital of personal experience in order to show you that I know something about the use of natural means for the restoration of the sick. God will work wonders for every one of us, if we work in faith, acting as we believe, that when we co-operate with Him, He is ready to do His part. I desire to do everything I can to lead my brethren to pursue a sensible course, in order that their efforts may be the most successful. Many who have gone down into the grave might today be living, if they had co-operated with God. Let us be sensible men and women in regard to these matters" (Ms50-1902).

(For a more thorough discussion of how James White recovered his health through agriculture, see Ms1-1867)

The Avondale Years

"I have planned what can be raised in different places. I have said, 'Here can be a crop of Alfalfa, there can be strawberries, here can be sweet corn and common corn; and this ground will raise good potatoes, while that will raise good fruit of all kinds.' So in imagination I have all the different places in a flourishing condition.

"No one need regret in reference to this land, for with the proper working, it will surprise the people in this section of the country" (Lt14-1894).

"Thousands of acres lie untouched, for no one attempts to work the land. They think it will yield nothing, but we know it will yield if properly cultivated....

"The school has twelve acres put into orchard; I have two acres in fruit trees. We shall experiment on this land, and if we make a success, others will follow our example.... When right methods of cultivation are adopted, there will be far less poverty than now exists.... We intend to give the people practical lessons upon the improvement of the land, and thus induce them to cultivate their land, now lying idle. If we accomplish this, we shall have done good missionary work" (Lt42-1895).

> *"We intend to give the people practical lessons upon the improvement of the land.... If we accomplish this, we shall have done good missionary work."*

"We have had to put all available help onto the land to prepare for the setting of our trees this week. If not set out this week, we must wait one year. I have been on the ground, using our two-horse team to go here and there and everywhere to save the time of the workers. We have pressed everyone into service we could command. Mr. Mosely came evening after the Sabbath. He is a gardener and furnished us the trees. He has a sample orchard at Orunbro twenty miles from here, and he will do his best to give us good fruit trees, for this will be a sample of what he can furnish for others. Every hand is busy today. The plow goes into the ground, and one follows the furrow to dig the holes and plant our trees of every variety. We have three acres cleared. The school planted three hundred trees yesterday. This is only a quarter of what they have on hand to plant.

"The light given me from the Lord is that whatever land we occupy is to have the very best kind of care and to serve as an object lesson to the Colonials of what the land will do if properly worked. So you see this has been a special, very important period of time for us" (Lt126-1895).

"All are gathering up flower roots for me to make my wilderness home blossom as the rose. Already we have many flowers, but I have plenty of space, and have set it apart for flowers. I wish that my home shall be made beautiful by the things of nature that God has created. Generally I call the attention of the children to these beautiful flowers, and tell them that these things are an expression of the love of God for them. I direct their mind from nature to nature's God. These lessons always seem to touch the hearts of the parents as well as the children. The pulpit is often festooned with flowers of every variety, and beautiful bouquets are brought me" (Lt59-1896).

"We are happily disappointed in the land here. We can now speak intelligently of what it can produce. On the school land and at "Sunnyside" White farm, we are giving object lessons of what can be done. I am so thankful to our heavenly Father that we can do this much. We are raising potatoes, corn, vegetables, and all are doing well. We are now enjoying some of the best string beans I have ever yet tasted. We raised these on our land. The seed, which was of a choice order, was planted last year, after supplying quite a large amount to our neighbors. I enjoy the retirement of my rural home" (Lt115-1896).

"We are trying to clear and work our land to show them in object lessons that if this land is worked properly it will yield its treasures. We worked our place just a little, for we came into the bush in August. We felled trees and made a clearing for an orchard, and planted oranges, lemons, peaches, apples, and apricots. We planted tomatoes, peas, beans, squash, cucumbers, melons, and carrots, and all these things grew and yielded abundantly. But we had only a little ground which we could work, and had no rain with the exception of light showers—two, I think, from Christmas until Christmas again. The impression has been made that nothing could be done with the land. We know better, and are proving the same. We hope the object lessons will be sufficient to set the people at work upon their own land.

"We have made some earnest efforts this year to show what can be done. We have our strong horses and plow, and we break up the land for our poor brethren that they may put in crops. All these experiments mean money out, but if we can help them to help themselves we will be doing a good work that the Lord will approve" (Lt132-1896).

"Everything in our home seems to be getting along. The farming is doing well. My flower garden is well stocked and yet I am gathering all kinds of roots, especially roses and lilies and carnations—pinks" (Lt161-1896).

> *"I determined to set my trees, even before the foundation of the house was built."*

"I determined to set my trees, even before the foundation of the house was built. We broke up only furrows, leaving large spaces unplowed. Here in these furrows we planted our trees the last of September, and lo, this year they were loaded with beautiful blossoms and the trees were loaded with fruit. It was thought best to pick off the fruit, although the trees had obtained a growth that seemed almost incredible. The small amount of fruit—peaches and nectarines—have served me these three weeks. They were delicious early peaches. We have later peaches—only a few left to mature as samples. Our pomegranates looked beautiful in full bloom. Apricots were trimmed back in April and June, but they threw up their branches and in five weeks by measurement had a thrifty growth of five and eight feet.

"If the Lord prospers us next year as He has done the past year, we will have all the fruit we wish to take care of, early and late. The early fruit comes when there is nothing else, so this is an important item. The peaches are rich and juicy and grateful to the taste. We have quince trees set out, and lemon, orange, apple, plum, and persimmon trees. We have even planted elderberry bushes. We planted our vineyard in June. Everything is flourishing and we shall have many clusters of grapes this season.

"We have a large strawberry bed which will yield fruit next season. We have a few cherry trees. The testimony is that the land is not good for cherries. But so many false, discouraging testimonies have been borne in regard to the land that we pay no attention to what they say. We shall try every kind of a tree. We have a large number of mulberry trees and fig trees of different kinds. This is not only good fruit land, but it is excellent in producing root crops and tomatoes, beans, peas, potatoes—two crops a season. All these good treasures that the land will yield have been brought in from Sydney and Newcastle and thousands of acres of land have been untouched because the owners say they will not raise anything. We have our farm as an object lesson.

"The school orchard is doing excellently well. If the land is worked it will yield its treasures, but weeds will grow, and those who own land will to exercise ambition to take these weeds out by the roots and give them no quarters. Deep plowing must be done. They let a few orange trees grow in the sod, also the lemons. We get the choicest, best oranges for three pence and two pence, ha' penny per dozen—six cents American money, and four and five cents per dozen for large, beautiful, sweet oranges.

"We have a large space of land devoted to ornamental trees and flowers. I have scoured the country for different plants, and I have a large bush of lemon verbena honeysuckle. We have a large variety of roses, dahlias, gladioli, geraniums, pinks, pansies, and evergreens. This must be a sample settlement, to tell what can be raised here.

"Brother Hughes told me he had a _____ tree for me, but Connell did not come for it. I was then at the post office near Mr. Hughes'. I said, 'Can I have it now?' He said, 'Yes.' He stepped into my sulky and we went to his place. I thought it took him a long time to get it, but when he came he had a tree ten feet high, a large stocky tree, and several smaller trees. The tree was in bloom. It has a flower some like a lilac, very fragrant. There I was alone, to take care of that tree and take it about two miles. But I did it. Had to get out and open two gates. I tended my tree, giving it every night a pail of water to drink. It never wilted, and this was last September. It is a flourishing tree. Everyone is astonished at the improvements we have made in so short a time.

"Just before my window, in my garden close by a beautiful fuchsia, a stalk of corn came up from the seed. We let it alone to grow. We took no pains to enrich it. In five weeks it grew eight feet and now, three weeks later, it has been stretching up until it measures in height, I believe, about thirteen feet, and it is still stretching upwards. It has the ears formed. The corn has tasseled. The ears are revealing the silk. I am seeing how this will develop.

"The garden is the exercise ground for my workers. Early and late the girls are at work in the garden when they are off duty. It is better for them, and more satisfactory than any exercise they can have. I could not persuade Marian to ride, could not get her from her writings; but now she has her interest awakened, and I have no fears but that she will get out of her chair and work in the garden. This garden of flowers is a great blessing to my girls, and they are working with the tomato raising, planting and caring for the tomatoes" (Lt162-1896, to Edson and Emma White).

"I immediately set to work on my garden men who were in need, some of them destitute of daily food. One man with a family of four children came to me and said that they had had nothing but squash to eat for a week. I gave them a cow; for they must have something for their children. We also plowed their land for them, my hired man doing the work. To another family I loaned a cow, that they might have milk for their children. I cannot see such poverty as this, without great pain of heart, for I know that there is enough in the world to sustain all if economy were practiced by those who have the means" (Ms55-1896).

> *"I arose at half past four a.m. [Monday]. At five I was at work spading up ground and preparing to set out my flowers."*

"I arose at half past four a.m. [Monday]. At five I was at work spading up ground and preparing to set out my flowers. I worked one hour alone, then Edith Ward and Ella May White united with me, and we planted our flowers. Then we set out twenty-eight tomato plants, when the bell rang for morning prayers and breakfast. I think I have received no harm from my vigorous exercise, but feel better for the work done....

"Tuesday morning I rose at half past three o'clock and again wrote a little in my diary. Worked some in the orchard, tying up the trees. A tuft of grass is put between the stake and the tree so that the tree shall not be marred.

"At five, Willie and I walked down to our garden, which is some distance from the house, and planted peas. We worked until seven a.m. and were prepared for our morning family prayer and for breakfast. I felt too weary to do more out of doors. We planned about many things that must be done on the ground" (Ms62-1896).

"We have located here on missionary soil, and we design to teach the people all round us how to cultivate the land. They are all poor because they have left their land uncultivated. We are experimenting, and showing them what can be done in fruit raising and gardening" (Lt33-1897).

"One year ago last July we entered this place with our horses and platform wagon without road or path. About the last of that month we brought our tents, and cleared a spot for two of them. In September my family tent was pitched and also my dining tent, and the men were set to work clearing. First we had a space cleared for buildings, then for our orchard. We had bullock teams come in and break up the sod in furrows, leaving the unbroken for a more convenient opportunity when money should be more plentiful. This lasted until the last of September, and in October trees were set in the place that had been well prepared for them. But we had no rain from September until December. Everything depended for water upon the water hole which lies near the orchard, near where water could be obtained for the trees. And last February and March we had the bullock teams complete the work of ploughing.

"Contrary to anything that I had expected, most of our peach trees were full of blossoms. In September, when we came home from camp meeting, we learned that the trees had been full of peaches, but that it had been thought wisdom to pick nearly all, leaving a few for samples. On November 25 I came home very sick from the conference in Ashfield, Sydney. A few of these early peaches had been saved for me, and they were very gratefully received. We have been picking the later peaches in January. These are the most beautiful in appearance that I have ever seen, being delicately and highly colored. And they are just as choice in taste as they are in appearance. I think I have never seen larger. Two of them weighed one pound. These same peaches are selling in Sydney at threepence each. If the Lord favors us next year, we will have at this time, beginning with December and lasting until the last of January, all the early peaches, nectarines, and apricots that we can eat and can.

"Our apples will not bear for a year or two. The trees were very small when set out. We have been living off our vegetables this year. Last we had but few tomatoes; but this year we have enough for ourselves and a good supply for our neighbors also. So we testify that the school land will yield abundantly this coming year if the Lord's blessing shall attend our labors. We are now eating sweet corn that this land has produced, and we enjoy it much. I wish I could pass around to Mother Wessels and your family the products of our experiments in farming this first year in the bush. The Lord has prospered us indeed" (Lt92-1897).

"We have not had to buy any garden produce this year. We have had plenty of potatoes, greens, green corn, green beans, tomatoes, and some grapes. We know how to prize these things, for we used to have to send to Parramatta for our vegetables and all our garden stuff, and when they reached us, they were so wilted and heated that at least half was not safe to use. Our garden has furnished our family of twelve, Willie's family of six, and Brother James family of ten. Brother James is our farmer. We have all the watermelons we can use. Some of them are delicious, and very large. We have squashes and real American pumpkins. We have pie plant, and if the Lord favors us, next year we shall have abundance of fruit, that we can can, from our own orchard. It is so much more palatable when we can eat it fresh from the trees" (Lt34-1898).

"My orange trees are full of blossoms. My peach and apricot trees are laden with fruit. If the Lord prospers us, we shall have fruit in abundance upon our trees this year.

"Three years ago the last of this month the trees were planted. Last year and the year before we had the most beautiful peaches and nectarines I ever tasted. Our mandarin trees bore abundantly last season, and are full of blossoms this year. Our passion fruit has borne continually through summer and winter for a year. My navel oranges, planted a year ago, are now in blossom. We have a very sightly flower garden. Some of the plants are in the very height of their glory. I wish you could see these things. This is the work my helpers in the literary line do. They work in the garden. Each has a spot of land, to care for and to beautify" (Lt84-1898).

"We now have a home upon the land, and what has been done speaks for itself. The land speaks for itself. The trees that were planted the last of September bore fruit in less than two years. The most beautiful peaches I have ever looked upon and most delicious to the taste, many of them weighing one half-pound each, have been produced on the land. From the first crop many of the peaches were picked off, for we feared that it would hurt the trees to let them bear so early. This last season our peach trees were so loaded with fruit that we had to prop up the branches. We have had all the vegetables we wanted for our own use, and have supplied the family of W. C. White and Brother James, our farm manager. The orchard at the school bore well, and the fruit was of a good flavor" (Ms62-1898).

"I have had to depend upon hired help, and unless I followed them critically they would rob me of time, and do their work in a slack, lazy, shiftless manner. I have had to pay out my money in wages and in seed for the cultivation of the land, which brought me no returns. I lost my seed, my income in produce, and tithe money that could have been brought into the treasury, because men were not diligent in business, fervent in spirit, serving the Lord.

"I was advised to employ a good, faithful man to care for my land, which I wished to cultivate in a Christian manner, so as to reveal the best symbol of what a farm should be in this country, where there are so many shiftless, lazy workmen who have never cultivated their land at all. We hired a good Christian farmer, and he has worked my land, which I am trying to make an object lesson to those who would rather beg than work. I know what a trial it is to have shiftless, indolent men, to whom you have to pay just as much in wages as to the man who has interest and fidelity, and puts religion into his work. I have just such a man [Brother James]" (Lt128-1899).

"We passed through many interesting experiences while in Australia. We helped establish a school from the foundation, going into the eucalyptus woods and camping while the trees were being felled, the grounds cleared, and the school-buildings erected....

"We did what we could to develop our land, and encouraged our neighbors to cultivate the soil, that they, too, might have fruit and vegetables of their own. We taught them how to prepare the soil, and what to plant, and how to take care of the growing produce. They soon learned the advantages of providing for themselves in this way" (Ms126-1902).

"I received your letter giving the particulars regarding your grounds and the cultivation of certain lines of fruit. While we were in Australia, we adopted the very plan you speak of—digging deep trenches and filling them in with dressing that would create good soil. This we did in the cultivation of tomatoes, oranges, lemons, peaches, and grapes.

"The man of whom we purchased our peach trees told me that he would be pleased to have me observe the way they were planted. I then asked him to let me show him how it had been represented in the night season that they should be planted. I ordered my hired man to dig a deep cavity in the ground, then put in rich dirt, then stones, then rich dirt. After this he put in layers of earth and dressing until the hole was filled. I told the nurseryman that I had planted in this way in the rocky soil in America. I invited him to visit me when these fruits should be ripe. He said to me, 'You need no lesson from me to teach you how to plant the trees.'

"Our crops were very successful. The peaches were the most beautiful in coloring and the most delicious in flavor of any that I had tasted. We grew the large yellow Crawford and other varieties, grapes, apricots, nectarines, and plums.

"A member of parliament who came to Cooranbong occasionally, and who had purchased the house in which we first lived in Cooranbong, visited our garden and orchard, and was greatly pleased with it. Several times we filled a large basket with fruit and took it to him and his wife at their home, and they were profuse in their thanks. After this they would always recognize us on the cars and speak of the great treat they had had in the fruit from our orchard. When they would visit us at our farm, they were always at liberty to eat all they wanted from the garden, and usually carried away a basket of fruit to their home. These favors brought us returns in several ways. Mention was made in the papers of the work being done by the students on the Avondale estate. And years afterward, when the terrible drought came, and the cattle were dying for want of pasture and food, the papers spoke of the wonderful exception to the drought to be found on the Avondale tract of land. They compared it to an oasis in the desert. Our crops were not cut off, and the farm flourished remarkably, notwithstanding the lack of rain" (Lt350-1907, To Edson and Emma White).

The Elmshaven Years

"This is a most beautiful location. The surroundings are lovely. Ornamental trees from various parts of the world, flowers, mostly roses of a large variety, an orchard containing a thousand prune trees which are bearing, another orchard nearer the house, and still another orchard of olive trees, are growing on the place. In the orchard near the house are apple trees, fig trees, apricots, cherries, and pears. We have sold our olives for fifty dollars a ton. I suppose there are not quite a ton on the trees. We have grapes in abundance, far more than we can handle. Next year we shall sell the crop for making sweet wine, which has a ready market" (Lt158-1900).

"When I returned to my home from the Conference [California camp meeting], several met me with the word, 'You will have no prunes this year. The buds were frozen on the trees, and the fruit is killed. I am so sorry.' 'Well,' I said, 'I thank God that it is not anything I have done that has brought this about. I thank the Lord that we shall not have the trouble and care of gathering the prunes.'

"Let us not complain. Let there be no complaints in our mouth" (Lt49-1901).

"The Lord is very good to us. Thus far, we have been favored with much fruit from our orchard. Last year we had scarcely any. We laid out much labor on the orchard, but the late frosts killed the fruit just as it was forming, so that we had very few prunes and very few apples. This year the prune trees are loaded, and we have had to buy large quantities of rope to tie up the branches, so that they would not break under their burden. In spite of our care, some of the branches have already broken....

"Sunday morning, Brother James, Sara, two of Brother James's children, and I rode seven miles up Howell mountain to get cherries—small, black ones, which were given us for the picking. Several others besides us were picking from the trees. The platform wagon was drawn under the trees, and Sara and I stood up on the seat, and in this way reached the cherries. I picked eight quarts. We took home a large box of the fruit, and put up thirty-seven quarts. So you see, Sister White is not decrepit yet" (Lt108-1902).

"This year we have been favored with an abundance of fruit. Our little patch of strawberries bore wonderfully—something as the corn bore last summer. The fruit was of an excellent flavor and very large, some of the berries measuring three and a half inches around, and one four inches.

"Our three large cherry trees were laden with cherries of a superior quality.... We put up about one hundred quarts of fruits from these trees.

From the first tree we sold enough to the Sanitarium to purchase several boxes of sour cherries, which we bottled. It is very desirable to have these to use with other fruit.

"About the time the cherries were all used, the loganberries ripened. In appearance these berries are somewhat like a large raspberry They are decidedly acid, but are a valuable fruit. We have had blackberries, also, from our own bushes; but for want of water, some of these berries are drying on the bushes. We are using the early apples now. For several weeks we have had applesauce on the table. Our family think much of this dish. We now have all the peaches we can eat. The grapevines are loaded. The prune trees are bearing so heavily that some of the branches are breaking" (Lt116-1902).

"My Dear Son Edson,—

"I wish you were here now, and that you could remain with us for a time to enjoy our fresh fruit and vegetables. I wish you could have come several weeks ago, at the beginning of the fruit season, and spent several months with us. We have been almost living on fruit. Early in the summer we had excellent strawberries. Later on we had cherries, loganberries, blackberries, and peaches. We are still eating and bottling peaches and have several trees of later varieties that have not ripened. For several weeks we have had all the apples that we could use. We are now enjoying the sweet corn grown in our garden. It is the sweetest corn that I ever tasted and is rich and nutritious. The tomatoes are just beginning to ripen.

"We have opportunity to buy all the fruit that we care to use, at low prices. Thus far, we have bought only blackberries and apricots for bottling, having sufficient of other kinds on our place. Blackberries of an excellent quality sell for three cents a pound; peaches, a cent and a half a pound. If you were here, you could dry some peaches. We have good facilities for drying fruit A furnace, a dryer, and large drying trays came with the place when we bought it.

"I am so pleased that we have so much fruit from my own place. There is still a chance for you to enjoy some of it. If Emma would come with you, I know she would enjoy it too. We now have apples, peaches, and nectarines. The early peaches are nearly all gone, but others are coming on, and we shall have all the peaches we can use until the end of the season. The plums are not yet ripe. Our tomatoes are ripening fast. The vineyard looks well, and there is promise of an abundant yield. Soon our prunes will be ripe enough to pick and dry These prunes are similar to the ones that we sent to you last year. If you could find room in your trunks to take some of them home, you would avoid having to pay much freight.

"I think that I will have a crate of blackberries put up for you, if you like them. Do you care for them?" (Lt130-1902).

"My place has brought me in nothing as yet; in fact, it has been some loss. We sold our last year's prune crop to a young man, a neighbor of ours. He bought largely from other prune orchards, and got more on his hands than he could manage. Then, too, the weather was very unfavorable for his drying operations, and he lost heavily. Of course, his creditors lost with him, and I among the rest. My loss was about five hundred dollars....

"The rain came early last year, and tons of my grapes rotted on the vines. These losses came at a time when I needed money very much. But I made no complaint; for this would not have helped the matter at all.

"Thus disappointment after disappointment has come to us. This year we have no apples or peaches on our place, and very few cherries. But we have much to be thankful for. The loganberry bushes are doing well. We had a few ripe strawberries, and on the land that I hire from the Sanitarium there was a very heavy crop of oats, which we shall use as winter feed for our horses and cows.

"We shall not have nearly so many prunes this year as we had last, but they will be larger, and will bring a good price. I am thankful to the Lord for every favor that I receive from His hand" (Lt111-1903, to P. T. Magan).

"For the past few months the farm and orchard have supplied a large part of our food, though some of the fruit trees, having borne a superabundance last year, bore hardly anything this year. At first we had strawberries and cherries. There were not so many of these as there were last year, but they were extra nice. Then came loganberries, and of these we had an abundance. We all enjoyed them exceedingly. We had a good crop of Early Rose potatoes, and they were as fine as any I have ever eaten.

"For three weeks we have been using tomatoes of our own raising. I thought them a long time ripening, but about three weeks ago I went to Healdsburg. We took some ripe tomatoes with us, and I was very glad that we did; for there was not a ripe tomato to be found over there.

"Brother Leininger has been given charge of a large apple orchard. The owner told him that he might give away all the windfalls. Brother Leininger told me of this and said that if I wished I could have all that I wanted of the apples that fell. We have been there several times to pick up apples, and thus we have been able to put up a large quantity of applesauce. The apples are wormy, but Sister Nelson prepares them carefully, cutting out all the decayed parts. We have apple sauce on the table every day.

"I find Sister Nelson to be a faithful, economical housekeeper. She has been very busy canning fruit and drying corn. The others have not been able to help her much; for they have all been busy on the writings. But Mrs. Nelson does not complain. She sees what needs to be done and does it. This is a great blessing.

"She has already canned one hundred and thirty-eight quarts of tomatoes, sixty quarts of loganberries, and seventy-five quarts of applesauce, besides cherries, peaches, and apricots. We hope to have two hundred quarts of tomatoes put up. We have nearly a bushel of sweet corn dried and have had sweet corn on the table nearly every day for two or three weeks.

"It seems wonderful that in this dry time—not a drop of rain has fallen for nearly six months—there can be such an abundance of tomatoes and sweet corn. To me this seems like a miracle; for the crops have not been watered, and there has been very little fog. I certainly cannot solve the problem of how, without a drop of rain, there can be so rich a harvest.

"The grapes are ripening fast. Oh, I wish that you and Brother Palmer and his family could be with us for a while. I know that you would enjoy grapes fresh from the vineyard.

"We do not know just what we shall do with our grapes. I wish that we could find a good market for them. But I shall not sell them to the wineries. We shall can a few, and perhaps make the rest into sweet wine. Last year we sold the whole crop to the Bakery, but they did not make proper provision to handle them, and many spoiled just as they were ready to pick.

"Our prunes this year are much larger than they were last year, but there are not nearly so many of them. We are drying them ourselves. Brother James' children have been gathering prunes for two or three days, and Brother James and Brother Packham dip the prunes and spread them on crates in the sun. We think that we shall be able to get a good price for them, because this year the prune crop everywhere is light.

"I think that I have told you how I lost on my prune crop last year. A young man, our nearest neighbor, bought the whole crop. He also bought largely from others who have prune orchards. He contracted for more than he could handle, and then the rain came early, and spoiled tons and tons of prunes. The young man lost everything and could not pay his creditors for the prunes that they had sold him. My loss was between five hundred and seven hundred dollars. I may possibly get fifty dollars after the young man's mother has sold this year's crop of prunes.

"Brother James wishes that you could have some of the prunes that he is now drying, and if we hear of any one going to the South, we shall try to send you some. The fresh prunes are very nice. Marian almost lives on them.

"A word or two more. I have on hand a large quantity of last year's prunes. I should be glad to give these to our people in the South. But I have not money to pay the cost of transportation. Have you any suggestion to make as to how these prunes could be sent South? Please mention this in your next letter" (Lt201-1903, to Edson and Emma White).

"For both breakfast and dinner today I have had all I desired of rich, sweet apricots. The peaches and apricots are delicious. Our peach trees are old, and we have only a few peaches this year; but we have new trees that will bear soon. I have been so hungry for fruit fresh from the trees that I could eat nothing else. We shall have these two kinds of fruit from now on.

"We have had a good crop of loganberries; they were very large and abundant. We did not raise strawberries this year, and we had very few cherries. Apples do not do well in our orchard. Our grapes are doing well. We have a few plants of a new mammoth blackberry, which we are going to try. We have been selling peas for more than a month, besides having an abundance for our own use. We have begun on the second crop now" (Lt222-1906, to Edson and Emma White).

"I wish you could be here with us to enjoy the products of our farm. We have had a good crop of loganberries. After using them freely for the table, canning, and making jelly, we have sold about two hundred dollars' worth. We have sold about fifty dollars' worth of green peas and are now gathering a second crop. They are very nice. Our new potatoes are excellent. They are dry, mealy, and very palatable.

"We are now using apple sauce from our early apples. These apples are small, but very nice. We have a few large cling-stone peaches, and others will ripen a little later. Today we are canning some luscious, fleshy blackberries. We have no apricots on the place, but we have purchased some that to me seem even richer and nicer than peaches. I have never tasted better apricots.

"We sent to Loma Linda for several gallons of clear, white, extracted honey. The bees collect this honey mostly from the orange and other fruit blossoms. If you will come, you may have all the honey you desire. I also have some grapefruit that was gathered from the trees at the Loma Linda Sanitarium.

"We had no strawberries this year, but we were able to get them in exchange for loganberries, box for box. A late frost killed about five hundred of our tomato plants soon after they were set out. But these have been replaced by others. The prospect is good for green corn. We had no cherries last year, and this year the cherry crop was very light. The frost must have injured the buds" (Lt240-1906, to Emma White).

"I would not be willing to exchange my farmer for any other person that I know of. I could not have a better helper than Brother James. When he first came here, he devoted his Sabbaths to holding meetings with unbelievers; he was always welcomed, for he explains the Scriptures in a clear and acceptable way. Now he finds that he must spend more time with his growing family....

"Brother James planted many loganberry vines; and when the fruit is ripe, he sells it. This year he has sold more than one hundred dollars' worth of fruit. When he came, the orchard was run down and had very little valuable fruit on it. He went to work and grafted our apple trees, and I wish you could see some of the apples we have had from our orchard this year. Some of them are larger than the Northern Spy. They are much like the Northern Spy in form, but I think I have never looked upon such perfection, both of form and color. I ate one and was delighted with its flavor. I wish I could send you some, but am afraid they will not bear transportation. The [Bell Flowers] come next in my estimation. These trees also, it was thought, would have to be grafted, or uprooted. We preferred to graft.

"We have not had such a good showing of delicious corn as we had last year. Last year we had enough to supply our neighbors. But although the supply has been limited, we have all enjoyed it while it lasted.

"Next come the grapes, which we are now enjoying. They are delicious. We will make no wine, for we find this does not pay, and we have not a large crop" (Lt284-1907, to Emma White).

"Our farm is cared for by Brother James, who labored for us in Australia. His family now numbers thirteen, including the parents. I do not think that one unpleasant word has ever passed between our two families in all our association together. Brother James has been quite successful in cultivating loganberries. Besides having all we needed for our own family, we sold last season one hundred dollars' worth of these berries. Of corn and peas we have raised enough for ourselves and our neighbors. The sweet corn we dry for winter use; then when we need it we grind it in a mill and cook it. It makes most palatable soups and other dishes" (Lt363-1907).

Bibliography

Special copyright notice: The source materials for this book are all to be found on the Ellen G. White website, http://egwwritings.org, copyright © 2015 Ellen G. White Estate, Inc.

Books:

AA	White, Ellen G. *The Acts of the Apostles.* Mountain View, CA: Pacific Press Publishing Association, 1911.
AY	_____. *An Appeal to the Youth.* Battle Creek, MI: Seventh-day Adventist Publishing Association, 1864.
CE	_____. *Christian Education.* Battle Creek, MI: International Tract Society, 1894.
COL	_____. *Christ Object Lessons.* Washington, DC: Review and Herald Publishing Association, 1900.

CT	_____. *Counsels to Parents, Teachers, and Students.* Mountain View, CA: Pacific Press Publishing Association, 1913.
CTBH	_____. *Christian Temperance and Bible Hygiene.* Battle Creek, MI: Good Health Publishing Co., 1890.
DA	_____. *The Desire of Ages.* Mountain View, CA: Pacific Press Publishing Association, 1898.
Ed	_____. *Education.* Mountain View, CA: Pacific Press Publishing Association, 1903.
FE	_____. *Fundamentals of Christian Education.* Nashville, TN: Southern Publishing Association, 1923.
GW	_____. *Gospel Workers.* Washington, DC: Review and Herald Publishing Association, 1915.
GW92	_____. *Gospel Workers.* Battle Creek, MI: Review and Herald Publishing Co., 1892.
HL	_____. *Healthful Living.* Battle Creek, MI: Medical Missionary Board, 1897.
LS80	_____. *Life Sketches of James White and Ellen G. White 1880.* Battle Creek, MI: Seventh-day Adventist Publishing Association, 1880.
MB	_____. *Thoughts from the Mount of Blessing.* Mountain View, CA: Pacific Press Publishing Association, 1896.
MH	_____. *The Ministry of Healing.* Mountain View, CA: Pacific Press Publishing Association, 1905.

Bibliography

PK		_____. *Prophets and Kings*. Mountain View, CA: Pacific Press Publishing Association, 1917.
PP		_____. *Patriarchs and Prophets*. Washington, DC: Review and Herald Publishing Association, 1890.
SA		_____. *A Solemn Appeal*. Battle Creek, MI: Seventh-day Adventist Publishing Association, 1870.
1SG		_____. *Spiritual Gifts*. Vol. 2. Battle Creek, MI: Seventh-day Adventist Publishing Association, 1860.
4aSG		_____. *Spiritual Gifts*. Vol. 4a. Battle Creek, MI: Seventh-day Adventist Publishing Association, 1864.
1SP		_____. *The Spirit of Prophecy*. Vol. 1. Battle Creek, MI: Seventh-day Adventist Publishing Association, 1870.
2SP		_____. *The Spirit of Prophecy*. Vol. 2. Battle Creek, MI: Seventh-day Adventist Publishing Association, 1877.
4SP		_____. *The Spirit of Prophecy*. Vol. 4. Battle Creek, MI: Seventh-day Adventist Publishing Association, 1884.
SpTEd		_____. *Special Testimonies on Education*. No imprint, 1897.
1T		_____. *Testimonies for the Church*. Vol. 1. Mountain View, CA: Pacific Press Publishing Association, 1868.

4T	_____. *Testimonies for the Church.* Vol. 4. Mountain View, CA: Pacific Press Publishing Association, 1881.
5T	_____. *Testimonies for the Church.* Vol. 5. Mountain View, CA: Pacific Press Publishing Association, 1889.
6T	_____. *Testimonies for the Church.* Vol. 6. Mountain View, CA: Pacific Press Publishing Association, 1901.
7T	_____. *Testimonies for the Church.* Vol. 7. Mountain View, CA: Pacific Press Publishing Association, 1902.

Pamphlets:

2Red	_____. *Redemption; or the Temptation of Christ in the Wilderness.*
PH085	_____. *Special Testimonies for the Battle Creek Church.*
PH117	_____. *Testimony for the Battle Creek Church.*
PH151	_____. *Selections from the Testimonies Setting Forth Important Principles Relating to Our Work in General, the Publishing Work in Particular, and the Relation of Our Institutions to Each Other.*
PH164	_____. *Words of Encouragement to Workers in the Home Missionary Field.*
SpTa04	_____. *Special Testimonies for Ministers and Workers.*
SpTb03b	_____. *Letters from Ellen G. White to Sanitarium Workers in Southern California.*

Bibliography

Periodicals:

Advocate *The Advocate.*

AUCR *Australasian Union Conference Record.*

BEcho *The Bible Echo.*

GCB *General Conference Bulletin.*

GH *The Gospel Herald.*

HM *The Home Missionary, The Missionary Magazine.*

HR *The Health Reformer.*

MMis *The Medical Missionary.*

PUR *Pacific Union Recorder.*

RH *The Review and Herald.*

SSW *Sabbath School Worker.*

ST *Signs of the Times.*

YI *The Youth's Instructor .*

Miscellaneous:

Lt Letters.

Ms Manuscripts.

SpM Spalding and Magan Collection.

We invite you to view the complete
selection of titles we publish at:

www.TEACHServices.com

Scan with your mobile
device to go directly
to our website.

Please write or email us your praises, reactions, or
thoughts about this or any other book we publish at:

P.O. Box 954
Ringgold, GA 30736

info@TEACHServices.com

TEACH Services, Inc., titles may be purchased in bulk for
educational, business, fund-raising, or sales promotional use.
For information, please e-mail:

BulkSales@TEACHServices.com

Finally, if you are interested in seeing
your own book in print, please contact us at

publishing@TEACHServices.com

We would be happy to review your manuscript for free.

www.ingramcontent.com/pod-product-compliance
Lightning Source LLC
Chambersburg PA
CBHW070552160426
43199CB00014B/2469